LETTER FROM A FRIEND

The initial publication and short-run printing of this book have been enabled by a generous donation from Upāsaka Guo Ke.

A Note on the Proper Care of Dharma Materials

Traditional Buddhist cultures treat books on Dharma as sacred. Hence it is considered disrespectful to place them in a low position, to read them when lying down, or to place them where they might be damaged by food or drink.

Letter from a Friend

A Bodhisattva's Advice to an Indian King
On Right Living and the Buddhist Path

The Suhṛllekha
An Epistle Composed for King Śatakarṇī
By Ārya Nāgārjuna (*circa* 200 CE)

THE THREE EARLIEST EDITIONS RENDERED FROM SANSKRIT BY:

Tripiṭaka Master Guṇavarman   (circa 425 CE)
Tripiṭaka Master Saṅghavarman   (circa 450 CE)
Tripiṭaka Master Yijing   (circa 675 CE)

English Translations by Bhikshu Dharmamitra

Kalavinka Press
Seattle, Washington
WWW.KALAVINKAPRESS.ORG

KALAVINKA PRESS
8603 39th Ave SW
Seattle, WA 98136 USA

WWW.KALAVINKAPRESS.ORG / WWW.KALAVINKA.ORG

Kalavinka Press is associated with the Kalavinka Dharma Association, a non-profit organized exclusively for religious educational purposes as allowed within the meaning of section 501(c)3 of the Internal Revenue Code. Kalavinka Dharma Association was founded in 1990 and gained formal approval in 2004 by the United States Internal Revenue Service as a 501(c)3 non-profit organization to which all donations are tax deductible.

Donations to KDA are accepted by mail and on the Kalavinka website where numerous free Dharma translations and excerpts from Kalavinka publications are available in digital format.

Copyright © 2005–2008 Bhikshu Dharmamitra. All Rights Reserved
Edition: Letter-SA-0608-1.0
ISBN: 978-1-935413-06-6
Library of Congress Control Number: 2009920874

PUBLISHER'S CATALOGING-IN-PUBLICATION DATA

Nagarjuna, 2nd c.
  [Long shu pu sa wei chan tuo jia wang shuo fa yao ji / Suhṛllekha. English translation.]
  [Quan fa ju wang yao ji / Suhṛllekha. English translation.]
  [Long shu pu sa quan jie wang song / Suhṛllekha. English translation.]
  Letter from a Friend. A Bodhisattva's Advice to an Indian King on Right Living and the Buddhist Path.
  Translations by Bhikshu Dharmamitra. – 1st ed. – Seattle, WA: Kalavinka Press, 2009.
    p. ; cm.
    ISBN: 978-1-935413-06-6
    Includes: text outlines; facing-page Chinese source text in both traditional and simplified scripts; notes. Other [Sanskrit-to-Chinese translating] authors: Tripitaka Master Gunavarman, Tripitaka Master Sanghavarman, Tripitaka Master Yijing.
  1. Mādhyamika (Buddhism)—Early works to 1800. 2. Bodhisattvas. 3. Spiritual life—Mahayana Buddhism. I. Gunavarman. II. Sanghavarman. III. Yijing. IV. Title
                                              2009920874
                                              0902

Cover and interior designed and composed by Bhikshu Dharmamitra.

Table of Contents

Acknowledgements	6
Abbreviation, Citation and Romanization Protocols	6
About the Chinese Text	6
Directory to the Guṇavarman Translation Edition	9
Directory to the Saṅghavarman Translation Edition	11
Directory to the Yijing Translation Edition	13
Introduction	15
The Guṇavarman Edition	23
Endnotes	59
The Saṅghavarman Edition	67
Endnotes	109
The Yijing Edition	117
Endnotes	159
Source Text Variant Readings	171
About the Translator	181

Directory to the Guṇavarman Translation Edition
(All outlining and section titles except main chapter titles originate with the translator.)

I. Introduction and Encouragement to Pay Due Attention	25
II. The Main Doctrinal Section	25
01. Six Recollections, Ten Goods, Quitting Intoxicants, Wrong Livelihood	25
02. The Six Perfections	25
03. Filial Respect for Parents	27
04. The Layperson's Eight-Precept *Upavāsa* Abstinence Rite	27
05. Abandonment of Faults	27
06. Diligence in Dispensing with Hate and Arrogance	29
07. The Three Kinds of Speech	29
08. Criteria for Evaluating Both Self and Prospective Associates	29
A. Four Types of Personal Destinies Linked to Brilliance or Darkness	29
B. Four Types of Persons Compared to a Mango's Ripeness	29
09. On Dealing with Desire	29
A. On Guarding the Mind	29
B. On the Hazards Inherent in Desire	31
C. On the Superior Valor in Controlling Desire	31
D. On the Unloveliness of the Body	31
10. In Praise of Contemplation-Based Insight, Wisdom, and Moral Virtue	31
11. Avoiding Eight Worldly Dharmas and Offenses Inspired by Others	33
12. On the Delayed Arrival of Karmic Retributions	33
13. On the Āryas' Seven Forms of Wealth	33
14. On Six Coarse Faults to Be Eliminated	33
15. In Praise of Being Easily Satisfied	33
16. On Moderation and Sensibility in Eating	35
17. Renounce Desires, Seek Nirvāṇa, Regulate the Body, Practice Upavāsa	35
18. Exhortation to Encourage Diligence in cultivating the Path	35
19. Four Immeasurable Minds and Cultivation of Dhyāna Absorptions	35
20. On the Necessity of Cultivating Counteractive Dharmas	35
21. On the Mitigating Effect of Predominant Goodness	37
22. Five Wrong Actions as Thieves; Five Roots as Sources of Good	37
23. Suffering, Its Origin, and Necessity of Right Views to Liberation	37
A. The Eight Sufferings; The Necessity of Right Views	37
B. The Four Inverted Views and the Harm They Wreak	37
C. Right and Wrong Views on the Aggregates	37
1. The Nonexistence of Any "Self" Linked to the Five Aggregates	37
2. On the Origins of the Aggregates	37
D. Three Fetters Impeding Liberation	39
24. The Necessity to Liberation of Self-Reliance	39

25. The Three Trainings: Moral Virtue; Dhyāna Concentration; Wisdom	39
26. The Station of Mindfulness with Respect to the Body	39
27. On the Circumstances Requisite for Cultivating the Path	41
28. Description of the Faults of Cyclic Existence	43
A. An Introductory General Description of Faults	43
B. The Gods	43
C. On the Unpredictability of Ostensibly Desirable States of Existence	45
D. The Hells	45
E. The Animals	49
F. The Hungry Ghosts	49
G. Rebirth Scenarios of the Gods	51
H. The Asuras	51
I. Summation on Cyclic Existence; Exhortation to Pursue the Path	51
29. Encouragement to Cultivate the Three Trainings and Seek Nirvāṇa	53
30. The Seven Limbs of Enlightenment	53
31. Avoidance of the Fourteen Indeterminate Dharmas	53
32. The Twelve-Fold Causal Chain, the Four Truths, and Eightfold Path	53
III. Concluding Exhortatory Section	53
01. Addendum on the Various Sorts of Candidates for Marriage	57
02. Final Closing Statement	57

Directory to the Saṅghavarman Translation Edition
(All outlining and section titles except main chapter titles originate with the translator.)

I. Introduction and Encouragement to Pay Due Attention — 69
II. The Main Doctrinal Section — 69
  01. The Six Recollections — 69
  02. Ten Good Karmic Deeds, Abandoning Intoxicants, Right Livelihood — 71
  03. The Six Perfections — 71
  04. Filial Respect for Parents — 71
  05. The Layperson's Eight-Precept *Upavāsa* Abstinence Rite — 73
  06. Abandonment of Faults — 73
  07. Non-Neglectfulness versus Neglectfulness — 73
  08. The Special Importance of Patience and Relinquishing Hatefulness — 73
  09. Three Kinds of Speech — 75
  10. Criteria for Evaluating Both Self and Prospective Associates — 75
    A. Four Types of Personal Destinies Linked to Brilliance or Darkness — 75
    B. Four Types of Persons Compared to a Mango's Ripeness — 75
  11. On Dealing with Desire — 77
    A. On Guarding the Mind — 77
    B. On the Hazards Inherent in Desire — 77
    C. On the Superior Valor in Controlling Desire — 77
    D. On the Unloveliness of the Body — 77
  12. In Praise of Contemplation-Based Insight, Wisdom, and Moral Virtue — 79
  13. Avoiding the Eight Worldly Dharmas and Offenses Inspired by Others — 79
  14. On the Delayed Arrival of Karmic Retributions — 79
  15. On the Āryas' Seven Forms of Wealth — 81
  16. On Six Coarse Faults to Be Eliminated — 81
  17. In Praise of Being Easily Satisfied — 81
  18. On the Various Sorts of Candidates for Marriage — 81
  19. On Moderation and Sensibility in Eating — 83
  20. Exhortation to Encourage Diligence and Mindfulness — 83
  21. Four Immeasurable Minds, Cultivation of the Dhyāna Absorptions — 83
  22. On the Mitigating Effect of Predominant Goodness — 83
  23. The Five Aggregates as Thieves; Five Roots and Powers as Guards — 83
  24. Suffering, Its Origin, and Necessity of Right Views to Liberation — 85
    A. The Eight Sufferings and the Basis for Their Arising — 85
    B. The Necessity of Right Views to Liberation — 85
    C. The Four Right Views versus the Four Inverted Views — 85
    D. Right and Wrong Views on the Aggregates — 85
      1. The Absence of Any "Self" Associated with the Five Aggregates — 85
      2. On the Origins of the Aggregates — 85
    E. Three Fetters Impede Liberation; Import of Wisdom, Self-Reliance — 85

25. THE THREE TRAININGS	87
26. THE STATION OF MINDFULNESS WITH RESPECT TO THE BODY	87
27. ON THE CIRCUMSTANCES REQUISITE FOR CULTIVATING THE PATH	89
28. DESCRIPTION OF THE FAULTS OF CYCLIC EXISTENCE	89
A. AN INTRODUCTORY GENERAL DESCRIPTION OF FAULTS	89
B. IMPERMANENCE AND REVERSIBILITY OF OSTENSIBLY DESIRABLE EXISTENCES	91
C. THE HELLS	93
D. THE ANIMALS	95
E. THE HUNGRY GHOSTS	97
F. THE GODS	99
G. THE ASURAS	99
H. SUMMATION ON CYCLIC EXISTENCE	99
29. EXHORTATION TO PURSUE THE PATH WITH VIGOR	99
30. EXHORTATION TO CULTIVATE THE THREE TRAININGS AND SEEK NIRVĀṆA	101
31. THE SEVEN LIMBS OF ENLIGHTENMENT	101
32. NECESSITY AND DECISIVE EFFECT OF MEDITATIVE ABSORPTION AND WISDOM	101
33. AVOIDANCE OF THE FOURTEEN INDETERMINATE DHARMAS	101
34. THE TWELVE-FOLD CHAIN OF CAUSES AND CONDITIONS	101
35. THE EIGHTFOLD PATH	103
36. THE FOUR TRUTHS: SUFFERING, ACCUMULATION, CESSATION, AND PATH	103
III. CONCLUDING EXHORTATORY SECTION	103

Directory to the Yijing Translation Edition
(All outlining and section titles except main chapter titles originate with the translator.)

I. Introduction and Encouragement to Pay Due Attention	119
II. The Main Doctrinal Section	121
01. The Six Recollections	121
02. The Ten Good Deeds, Abandonment of Intoxicants, Right Livelihood	121
03. The Six Perfections	121
04. Filial Respect for Parents	121
05. The Layperson's Eight-Precept *Upavāsa* Abstinence Rite	123
06. Abandonment of Faults	123
07. Diligence versus Negligence	123
08. On the Special Importance of Patience and Relinquishing Enmity	123
09. Three Kinds of Discourse	125
10. Criteria for Evaluating Both Self and Prospective Associates	125
A. Four Types of Personal Destinies Linked to Brilliance or Darkness	125
B. Four Types of Persons Compared to a Mango's Ripeness	125
11. On Dealing with Desire	127
A. On Guarding the Mind	127
B. On the Hazards Inherent in Desire	127
C. On the Superior Valor in Controlling Desire	127
D. On the Impurity of the Body	127
12. In Praise of Contemplation-Based Insight, Wisdom, and Moral Virtue	127
13. Avoiding Eight Worldly Dharmas and Offenses Inspired by Others	129
14. On the Delayed Arrival of Karmic Retributions	129
15. On the Āryas' Seven Forms of Wealth	129
16. On Six Coarse Faults to Be Eliminated	129
17. In Praise of Reduced Desires	131
18. On the Various Sorts of Candidates for Marriage	131
19. On Moderation and Sensibility in Eating	131
20. Exhortation to Encourage Diligence and Mindfulness	131
21. Four Immeasurable Minds and Cultivating the Dhyāna Absorptions	131
22. On the Necessity of Cultivating Counteractive Dharmas	133
23. On the Mitigating Effect of Predominant Goodness	133
24. On the Destructive Power of the Five Hindrances	133
25. The Five Root-Faculties, Powers, and Summits	133
26. Suffering, Its Origin, and Necessity of Right Views to Liberation	133
A. The Eight Sufferings	133
B. The Necessity of Right Views to Liberation	135
C. The Four Right Views versus the Four Inverted Views	135
D. Right and Wrong Views on the Aggregates	135
1. The Nonexistence of Any "Self" Linked to the Five Aggregates	135

2.	On the Origins of the Aggregates	135
E.	Three Fetters Impeding Liberation	135

27. Necessity of Self-Reliance, Learning, Moral Virtue, and Meditation — 135
28. The Three Trainings — 137
29. The Station of Mindfulness with Respect to the Body — 137
30. On the Circumstances Requisite for Cultivating the Path — 139
31. Description of the Faults of Cyclic Existence — 139

A.	An Introductory General Description of Faults	139
B.	Impermanence and Reversibility of Ostensibly Desirable Existences	141
C.	The Hells	143
D.	The Animals	147
E.	The Hungry Ghosts	147
F.	The Gods	149
G.	The Asuras	149
H.	Summation on Cyclic Existence	151

32. Exhortation to Pursue the Path with Vigor — 151
33. Encouragement to Cultivate the Three Trainings and Seek Nirvāṇa — 151
34. The Seven Limbs of Enlightenment — 151
35. Necessity and Decisive Effect of Skill in Meditation and Wisdom — 151
36. Avoidance of the Fourteen Indeterminate Dharmas — 151
37. The Twelve-Fold Chain of Causes and Conditions — 153
38. The Eightfold Path — 153
39. The Four Truths: Suffering, Accumulation, Cessation, and Path — 153

III. Concluding Exhortatory Section — 155

Introduction

General Introduction to the *Suhṛllekha*

Ārya Nāgārjuna's *Letter from a Friend* (*Suhṛllekha*) is a short discourse composed in the form of a royal-advisory letter presented by a spiritual teacher to the king of his country. It is unknown precisely to which of several similarly-titled Sātavāhana monarchs known as Śatakarṇī that Ārya Nāgārjuna addressed the *Letter*. The king in question likely held sway in the southeast Indian city of Amaravati in Andhra Pradesh sometime during the first quarter of the first millennium CE. (The Sātavāhana Empire lasted at most some 450 years, from roughly 230 BCE to approximately 220 CE.)

On the Author of this Text

The author of this treatise, Ārya Nāgārjuna lived in Southern India in the early years of the first millennium CE. He is recognized by followers of all Northern School Buddhist traditions as one of the foremost advocates of the Mahāyāna path dedicated to universal spiritual liberation and realization of buddhahood. Nāgārjuna championed this altruistic path as ultimately of a higher order than the individual-liberation paths idealizing personal escape from suffering through the enlightenment of arhats or pratyekabuddhas.

The works of Ārya Nāgārjuna are unsurpassed in their ability to clarify the fundamental tenets, aims, and right practice of the bodhisattva's universal-liberation path. Details about his life and the texts he composed are, due to constraints of space, beyond the scope of this introduction. The reader may look to the introduction to my translation of Nāgārjuna's *Strand of Jewels* (*Ratnāvalī*) for a few more relevant comments. Alternatively, one may choose to explore this topic through perusal of secular buddhology's endless conjectures about Nāgārjuna's life and works.

On the Especially Valuable Qualities of This Text

Although Ārya Nāgārjuna has certainly written many other texts which are more metaphysically abstruse and doctrinally encyclopedic than this *Letter from a Friend*, this text is in fact one of the most accessible, appropriate, and useful basic Buddhist instruction manuals available to the Western student of Dharma. It is especially valuable because it presents in a very short text practical advice from an acknowledged master, practical advice which is equally useful to both layperson and monastic. This letter of spiritual counsel from Nāgārjuna himself emphasizes the most important aspects of the Buddhist Path: right living, right Buddhist practice, and the right doctrinal bases for developing world-transcending moral virtue, contemplative practice, and wisdom.

On the Surviving Editions and Their Origins

Although there are apparently no surviving traces of the original Sanskrit text of Ārya Nāgārjuna's *Suhṛllekha* or *Letter from a Friend*, we do have four significantly-varying editions extant in secondary languages, three preserved in the Chinese canon (T32.1672-4), and one preserved in Tibetan (TP-5409, duplicated as TP-5682). There is also an Indian commentary translated into Tibetan (TP-5690).

Dating on all of these materials involves some uncertainty with dating of the Tibetan texts being least clear. (It is probably safe to say the Tibetan translations were made between 800-1200 CE.)

As for the translation dates from Sanskrit of the three Chinese editions featured in this volume, Takakusu provisionally assigns them as follows (*A Record of the Buddhist Religion*, p. 158):

T32.1672, by Tripiṭaka Master Guṇavarman:	431 CE
T32.1673, by Tripiṭaka Master Saṅghavarman:	434 CE
T32.1674, by Tripiṭaka Master Yijing:	673 CE

On Similarities to and Differences from the *Ratnāvalī*

Students of Ārya Nāgārjuna's works will already be familiar with another royal-advisory discourse (*rāja-parikathā*), the immensely-important *Ratnāvalī*, also composed in the form of discourse presented to one of the Sātavāhana monarchs ruling in Amaravati. The similarities between the *Suhṛllekha* and the *Ratnāvalī* are fewer than one might expect, for they differ markedly in the range and metaphysical abstruseness of doctrinal content while also apparently being composed for kings at different stages of path development.

A thorough study of the two texts makes it seem probable that, if they were not written for two entirely different kings, they were at minimum composed for the same king at very different stages in his study of the Path. However, a close comparative reading of the two texts reveals internal circumstantial evidence contradicting this latter theory, for it seems highly likely from such evidence that both texts were composed for relatively young kings still at the beginning stages of their careers in state governance.

Of particular importance are the numerous examples of categorical differences in doctrinal content between the *Suhṛllekha* and the *Ratnāvalī*, including (but not limited to) the following:

1) Whereas the *Suhṛllekha* does indeed mention Mahāyāna topics such as the six perfections and Avalokiteśvara Bodhisattva (in the Yijing edition, Amitābha Buddha is mentioned as well), its greatest emphasis is on the more basic Buddhist practices most essential to individual liberation. In marked contrast, the *Ratnāvalī* devotes itself almost entirely to a bodhisattva's universal-liberation doctrines, aspirations, and practice.

2) Although the *Ratnāvalī* does in fact encourage renunciation for sense-bound enslavement to cyclic existence, it emphasizes altruistic bodhisattva works during a very long course of countless lifetimes in the very midst of cyclic existence. In marked contrast, and as well befits a less heroically-inclined target audience, the *Suhṛllekha* devotes a great deal of effort to articulating the direct-experience rationales for developing a strong aversion to uncontrolled coursing in cyclic existence while only peripherally mentioning the self-sacrificing details of the bodhisattva career.

Most noteworthy in this respect are the *Suhṛllekha* passages reserved for cataloguing the inescapable sufferings associated with each level of cyclic existence from the hells on up to the heavens. As one might expect, due attention is paid to the baseless nature of loveliness imputations commonly associated with members of one's opposite gender. Additionally, the eight major categories of suffering and the rarity of encountering a human rebirth well-suited to cultivating the Path are also discussed.

3) The *Suhṛllekha* does make a point of noting the indispensability of right view to spiritual liberation and so does mention essential basic related topics such as: the thirty-seven wings of enlightenment, the four inverted views, absence of an inherently-existent "self" anywhere in the five aggregates, the three fetters impeding liberation, the twelve-fold causal chain, avoidance of the fourteen indeterminate dharmas wedded to useless discourse, and the three trainings. Still, the depth of discussion is not nearly so thoroughgoing and abstruse as we find in the *Ratnāvalī*. Also, the *Ratnāvalī* really does go hammer-and-tongs at demonstrating virtually the

entire range of exemplary illustrations of the doctrine of emptiness, whereas the *Suhṛllekha* barely touches on this essential doctrine so crucial to right Mahāyāna realization and practice.

At first glance, it might be tempting to attribute the above-listed differences between these two texts to inevitable condensation factors at play in very short works such as the *Suhṛllekha*. (At 500 *ślokas*, the *Ratnāvalī* is more than four times the length of the 120-odd *ślokas* found in each of the *Suhṛllekha's* four editions.) However, this would still not adequately explain the major differences which extend more deeply to matters of widely-varying doctrinal emphasis, tenor, and target audience.

On Possibly Different Authorship of the *Suhṛllekha* and *Ratnāvalī*

This matter of "target audience" mentioned directly above explains why, doctrinally-speaking, it is not reasonable merely on grounds of the less-exalted version of doctrine articulated in the *Suhṛlekkha*, to propose different authorship to the *Suhṛllekha* and the *Ratnāvalī*. The bodhisattva guru is well aware of the need to tailor teaching stratagems to the faculties of the student.

One need only reference the counsel to adopt varying levels of teaching stratagems recommended in both the *Ratnāvalī* and the *Bodhisaṃbhāra Śāstra* to realize why a single bodhisattva-path guru would adopt very basic teachings for one student and extremely challenging and abstruse teachings for another. It would be an entirely commonplace scenario for a guru to adopt only a basic individual-liberation teaching stratagem in the early phases of teaching one individual of only limited spiritual capacities whilst on the very same day employing refined teachings demanding superhuman resolve and far-reaching spiritual vision in the instruction of a student possessing marvelously well-developed bodhisattva-path capacities.

It is on this basis that I tend to dismiss as merely conjectural any doctrinally-rooted arguments proposing that the *Suhṛllekha* and the *Ratnāvalī* might have been composed by different hands.

Śloka Numbering in the Chinese Editions

Specialists and original-language students of these texts will know from their reading experience that, although there may be some exceptions, it is the norm for the Chinese translations produced by both Indian and Chinese translators to not include any sort of *śloka* numbering. In fact, translations into Chinese very often run the *ślokas* together and thus entirely do away with any boundaries between *ślokas*. As one will note from examination of my translations of these three texts, it was also not uncommon at all for particular translators to render doctrinally dense stanzas with more lines and doctrinally very simple stanzas with fewer lines.

Sanskrit source texts perhaps varied somewhat as to whether they retained scribal demarcations or rather simply let the structure of the Sanskrit speak for itself. Apparently, even in more complex texts, it was not particularly uncommon for helpful apparatuses to be entirely absent from Sanskrit manuscripts with the result being that there was no linguistic demarcation between extensive comments by an exegete and the root-text passage upon which it commented. In cases of that sort, the Chinese translation process often involved adding clear demarcations and detailed titles, subtitles, headings, and subheadings.

In any case, specifically because English translations of Tibetan editions of the Suhṛllekha have carefully preserved a numbering schema for the 123 ślokas of their text, I have inserted a moderately-accurate *śloka*-numbering schema in all three of my *Suhṛllekha* translations, including also the corresponding Tibetan *śloka* numbers (where such correlation is possible at all), this to facilitate investigative comparison of the various editions and also to provide additional convenience for Dharma students and practitioners who have so far only studied this text from the standpoint of the Tibetan edition.

On Other Elements Added by the Translator

The reader will notice the presence of an outline structure containing headings and subheadings both in the tables of contents and also in the translations themselves. These elements were created by the English-language translator as a means to assist more ready access to the structure of the texts by the reader. This outlining apparatus is only approximate and was created more-or-less "on-the-fly" while I produced each of the translations. Consequently I cannot claim to have precisely captured the more subtle terrains of Ārya Nāgārjuna's text. It would not surprise me in the least if readers were to find bases for further refinements of my outlining heads and sub-heads which are, after all, intended solely to act as a rough guide to the structure of the text.

Additionally, I've included on verso pages the source-language texts in both simplified-character and traditional-character scripts. These apparatuses are included for two primary reasons:

First, it may be helpful for Dharma students and specialists who have taken the time to develop Chinese-language skills to have ready access to the source-language when contemplating difficult passages.

Second, there are a fair number of Dharma students today who, native speakers or not, can read the Chinese moderately well, but who still find it useful to have some assistance in dealing with Sino-Buddhist technical terms not found anywhere in the modern Chinese lexicon. Facing-page English allows easy access to correct understanding of technical terms while also offering cues on the meaning of relatively obscure Chinese passages couched in the sometimes less-familiar Classical Chinese literary style.

Why Translate All Three Chinese Editions Instead of Just One?

This is certainly a question which occurred to me right away when first pondering a *Suhṛllekha* translation project. Closer study of all four surviving editions of the text made it obvious to me that the differences in the texts were so marked that the most meaningful contribution to study of this text by modern-day Dharma students would consist in going ahead and rendering into English all three Sanskrit-to-Chinese editions.

There are certainly differences in all of the translations on crucial elements. These involve ideas being included in one translation but not in all or any of the others.

There are also other significant variations worth pondering, among which, for example, we have Tripiṭaka Master Yijing's preference for a more elegant literary style almost certainly more appealing to the well-educated Chinese reader but, unfortunately, also somewhat more amenable to generating ambiguity. In technical documents such as those concerned with teaching details of Dharma, any unnecessary ambiguity increases the likelihood that any given reader might choose one valid Chinese reading over another and hence miss the intent of the Sanskrit original which in fact intended to convey one and only one meaning for the given phrase or passage.

There are yet other factors discoverable through examining multiple translations, factors perhaps implicitly freighted with a degree of historical and doctrinal significance. Take for instance Tripiṭaka Master Guṇavarman's very condensed statement on factors to consider in choosing a wife (included more-or-less like an "addendum" as the very last stanza in his edition). This stands in marked contrast to the case obtaining with the other three editions (including the Tibetan) wherein discussions of ideal and disastrous marriage partners for a monarch are both much more detailed and also appear to be integral to an earlier section of the text.

Noting that Tripiṭaka Master Guṇavarman was in fact an arhat whose extraordinary powers were well known in his time (walking on mud without leaving tracks, knowing when Buddha-hall bells were being struck even when still miles away from the monastery, etc.), one wonders if his edition of the *Suhṛllekha* might have been a somewhat different version more commonly encountered in Indian monasteries more focused on the individual-liberation arhatship path. On the other hand, it might perhaps have occurred that in all subsequent editions, we have a case of someone's commentary becoming intentionally or unintentionally integrated into the text, thus making the treatment of the "royal marriage" topic much more detailed than Ārya Nāgārjuna might ever have intended.

Translation of all extant editions also contributes a little more "grist" for discussions on the degree of accuracy preserved in orally-transmitted texts. Limitations of space preclude pursuing that topic in this introduction.

On the Meaning of the *Suhṛllekha* Title

I have noticed that the currently circulating English translations made from the Tibetan edition of the *Suhṛllekha* tend to translate this work's title as "Letter *to* a Friend" (in contrast to my choice of "Letter *from* a Friend"). This may or may not involve some artifact in the way the title was translated from Sanskrit into Tibetan. (The Sanskrit itself appears to be "neutral" on this issue.)

Having noted this seemingly minor point, I still do think it worth pointing out that an entirely standard feature of Buddhist doctrine incidentally bears very directly on what might or might not constitute a valid rendering of Nāgārjuna's intent: Although the king in question here may indeed have been a "friend" of Nāgārjuna in the loose sense of the term, it is Nāgārjuna who adopts in this letter of instruction the role of the "good spiritual friend" (*kalyāṇa-mitra*) or "spiritual guide."

Additionally, it is Nāgārjuna who is the already-enlightened *ārya*, not the King, for the King is, no different from the rest of us, a mere "foolish common person" (*pṛthag-jana*) who, by definition, is still vulnerable to being subverted by his own constantly-varying affections and aversions. As is often pointed out in Buddhist doctrinal literature, it is a person who has become an *ārya* and *only* a person who has become an *ārya* whom one can rely upon to act as one's friend throughout this and all future lives. This is because, by definition, only an *ārya* has already reached that level of enlightenment from which he can never fall back in either this or future lives. (This stage is synonymous with "stream-entry" on the individual liberation path and, at the latest, eighth-stage bodhisattvahood on the universal-liberation path.)

The king, "friend" that he might appear to be for the time being, might just as easily change into a deadly enemy with a change of circumstances (say, were he to convert to another religion, for instance) or a change of lifetimes. Hence my distinctly different translation choice for the English rendering of *Suhṛllekha*.

In Summary

Ārya Nāgārjuna's *Letter from a Friend* is an especially accessible and concise outline of the most essential elements of the Buddhist path. If studied with due respect and care, it should serve well as a source of constant and trustworthy spiritual counsel for any student of the Dharma. This being the case, I hope that this three-edition volume may enjoy wide circulation among Buddhist practitioners and others wishing to explore more deeply the works of Nāgārjuna.

Suggestions for improvements in this translation from clergy, scholars, or Dharma students may be forwarded via website email and will certainly be very much appreciated.

Bhikshu Dharmamitra
Spring, 2008

Letter From a Friend (The *Suhṛllekha*)
Edition One: The Guṇavarman Translation

The Dharma Essentials Verses
Composed by Nāgārjuna Bodhisattva for King Śatakarṇi

Translated by the Kashmiri Tripiṭaka Master Guṇavarman
During the Early Song Dynasty (circa 431 CE)

English Translation by Bhikshu Dharmamitra

龙树菩萨
为禅陀迦王说法要偈

宋[1]罽宾三藏求那跋摩译

禅陀迦王应当知
生死苦恼多众过
悉为无明所覆障
吾欲为彼兴利益

譬如刻画造佛像
智者见之宜恭敬
我依如来说正法
大王亦应深信受

汝虽先闻牟尼言
今若听受转分别
犹如华池色清净
月光[2]垂照逾晖显

佛说六念当修习
所谓三宝施戒天
修行十善净三业
离酒放逸及邪命

观身命财速危朽
应施福田济穷乏
施为坚牢无与等
最为第一亲近者

简体字

Letter from a Friend[1]

The Dharma Essentials Verses
Composed by Nāgārjuna Bodhisattva for King Śatakarṇī

Translated by the Early Song Kashmiri Tripiṭaka Master Guṇavarman

I. Introduction and Encouragement to Pay Due Attention

1 (T2)
King Śatakarṇī should realize
The many faults associated with birth-and-death's bitter afflictions.
Everyone is covered over and obstructed by ignorance.
I wish for their sakes to allow benefit to flourish.

2 (T2)
Just as when an image of the Buddha made by carving or painting,
Beheld by the wise, appropriately inspires them to reverence,
Just so, as I rely on the Tathāgata to explain right Dharma,
The Great King too should be inspired to deep faith and acceptance.

3 (T3)
Although you may have previously heard the words of the Muni,[2]
If you now listen and absorb them, your discernment shall increase.
This is comparable to a lotus pool's appearance of purity—
When moonlight falls upon it, it shines forth ever more radiantly.

II. The Main Doctrinal Section
   01. Six Recollections, Ten Goods, Quitting Intoxicants and Wrong Livelihood

4 (T4-5)
The Buddha declared that one should cultivate the six recollections,[3]
Namely the Three Jewels,[4] giving,[5] moral virtue, and the heavens,
While cultivating ten good deeds,[6] purifying three types of karma,[7]
And abandoning intoxicants as well as wrong livelihood.

   02. The Six Perfections

5 (T6)
Observing that one's physical life and wealth swiftly deteriorate,
One should give to fields of merit and rescue the poor and destitute.[8]
Giving is unmatched in its durability.
It is the foremost among all of one's close companions.[9]

勤修净戒除瑕秽 亦莫悕求愿诸有 譬如大地[3]殖众物 戒亦如是生诸善	勤修淨戒除瑕穢 亦莫悕求願諸有 譬如大地[3]殖眾物 戒亦如是生諸善
修忍柔和舍瞋恚 佛说是行最无上 如是精进及禅智 具此六行超生死	修忍柔和捨瞋恚 佛說是行最無上 如是精進及禪智 具此六行超生死
若能在家孝父母 此即名为胜福田 现世流布大名称 未来福报转无量	若能在家孝父母 此即名為勝福田 現世流布大名稱 未來福報轉無量
杀盗婬欺耽荒酒 雕床高广及香熏 讴歌倡伎过时食 如斯众恶宜远离 若少时[4]间修此戒 必受天乐升涅盘	殺盜婬欺耽荒酒 雕床高廣及香熏 謳歌倡伎過時食 如斯眾惡宜遠離 若少時[4]間修此戒 必受天樂昇涅槃
悭嫉贪欲及谄伪 诳惑颠倒与懈怠 如此众恶不善法 大王当观速弃舍	慳嫉貪欲及諂偽 誑惑顛倒與懈怠 如此眾惡不善法 大王當觀速棄捨
端正尊豪及五欲 当知危朽若泡沫 莫恃若斯不坚法 憍逸自恣生诸苦 欲长诸善证甘露 应当远离如弃毒	端正尊豪及五欲 當知危朽若泡沫 莫恃若斯不堅法 憍逸自恣生諸苦 欲長諸善證甘露 應當遠離如棄毒
简体字	正體字

6 (T7)
Diligently cultivate pure precepts to be rid of faults and defilements.
Also, do not aspire to abide in any of the realms of existence.
Just as the great earth supports the birth of the many creatures,
So too, in like fashion, do moral precepts produce all forms of good.

7 (T8, 15)
Cultivate gentle harmony with patience, relinquishing hatefulness.
The Buddha proclaimed this practice as the most superior.[10]
In like fashion, develop vigor as well as dhyāna and wisdom.
By perfecting these six practices, one steps beyond birth and death.

03. Filial Respect for Parents
8 (T9)
If one is able as a householder to show filial respect for one's parents,
Then this in itself serves as a supreme field for the growth of merit.[11]
In this present life, a great reputation will spread afar
While future karmic rewards from this merit become incalculable.[12]

04. The Layperson's Eight-Precept Upavāsa Abstinence Rite
9 (T10-11)
Killing, stealing, sexual relations,[13] deception, indulging intoxicants—
Sleeping in ornate beds, high and broad, and using perfumes,
Singing, attending performances, and eating past the correct time—
It is fitting to abandon the many such unwholesome actions.[14]
If one cultivates these moral precepts even for a short time,[15]
One is surely destined for celestial happiness and ascent to nirvāṇa.[16]

05. Abandonment of Faults
10 (T12)
Miserliness, hatefulness, covetousness, lust, flattery and falseness—
Deceptiveness, inverted views, and indolence—
The many sorts of evil and unwholesome dharmas such as these
Are such as the Great King should reflect upon and swiftly cast off.

11 (T13)
As for handsomeness, honorable caste, and the five objects of desire,[17]
One should realize those things are as vulnerable to ruin as sea-foam.
Don't rely on such nondurable dharmas as these,
For arrogantly indulging them generates all manner of sufferings.
If one wishes to develop goodness and gain the sweet dew ambrosia,
One should abandon them just as one would cast aside poison.

简体字	正體字
有能精勤舍[5]瞋慢 譬如除云显秋月 犹如指鬘与难陀 亦如差摩贤圣等	有能精勤捨[5]瞋慢 譬如除雲顯秋月 猶如指鬘與難陀 亦如差摩賢聖等
如来说有三种语 入意真实虚妄言 入意如花实犹蜜 虚[6]妄鄙恶若粪秽 应当修习前二言 速宜除断虚妄者	如來說有三種語 入意真實虛妄言 入意如花實猶蜜 虛[6]妄鄙惡若糞穢 應當修習前二言 速宜除斷虛妄者
从明入明四种法 王当分别谛思惟 二种入明是应修 若就痴冥当速舍	從明入明四種法 王當分別諦思惟 二種入明是應修 若就癡冥當速捨
菴婆罗果四种变 人难分别亦如是 当以智慧深观察 若实贤善宜亲近	菴婆羅果四種變 人難分別亦如是 當以智慧深觀察 若實賢善宜親近
虽见女人极端严 当作己母姊女想 设起贪欲染爱心 应当正修不净观	雖見女人極端嚴 當作己母姊女想 設起貪欲染愛心 應當正修不淨觀
是心躁动宜禁制 如防身命及珍宝 欲心若起应惊怖 犹畏刀剑恶兽等	是心躁動宜禁制 如防身命及珍寶 欲心若起應驚怖 猶畏刀劍惡獸等

06. Diligence in Dispensing with Hate and Arrogance

12 (T14)

When able to diligently dispensing with hatefulness and arrogance,
This compares to when clouds disperse, revealing the autumn moon.
Such changes are like those of Aṅgulimāla[18] and Sundarananda,[19]
Or like that of Śamā,[20] who rivaled even the Worthies and Āryas.[21]

07. The Three Kinds of Speech

13 (T18)

The Tathāgata stated that there are three types of discourse:
That appealing to the mind, the truthful, and that which is false.
Speech appealing to the mind is like flowers, the true is like honey,
And the false is base, evil, and comparable to fecal filth.
One should cultivate the first two kinds of speech
And, as is fitting, quickly cut off whatever is false.

08. Criteria for Evaluating Both Self and Prospective Associates

A. Four Types of Personal Destinies Linked to Brilliance or Darkness

14 (T19)

The four dharmas involving leaving or proceeding into brilliance
Are such as the King should distinguish and carefully contemplate.
One should cultivate the two leading forth into brilliance.
Those leading into delusion's darkness should be swiftly abandoned.

B. Four Types of Persons Compared to a Mango's Ripeness

15 (T20)

Just as with the four states found in the ripening of a mango,
The difficulty of making distinctions among people is much the same.
One should resort to wisdom and deep contemplative investigation.
It may be fitting to draw near the genuinely worthy and good.

09. On Dealing with Desire

A. On Guarding the Mind

16 (T21)

Although one may behold an extremely beautiful and stately woman,
One should reflect on her as with one's mother, sister, or daughter.
If one generates lustful and defiled thoughts,
One should cultivate correctly the contemplation of impurity.

17 (T22)

If such thoughts become restive, it is fitting to control them
Just as one would do in guarding one's life or one's precious jewels.
If desire-ridden thoughts arise, one should be alarmed
Just as one feels fear encountering drawn swords or dreadful beasts.

简体	正體
欲为无利如怨毒 如此之言牟尼说 生死轮迴过狱缚 应当勤修求解脱	欲為無利如怨毒 如此之言牟尼說 生死輪迴過獄縛 應當勤修求解脫
六入躁动驰诸境 应当摄持莫放逸 若能如是摄诸根 胜于勇将摧强敌	六入躁動馳諸境 應當攝持莫放逸 若能如是攝諸根 勝於勇將摧強敵
是身不净九孔流 无有穷已若河海 薄皮覆蔽似清净 犹假璎珞自庄严 诸有智人乃分别 知其虚诳便弃舍	是身不淨九孔流 無有窮已若河海 薄皮覆蔽似清淨 猶假瓔珞自莊嚴 諸有智人乃分別 知其虛誑便棄捨
譬如疥者近猛焰 初虽暂悦后增苦 贪欲之想亦复然 始虽乐着终多患	譬如疥者近猛焰 初雖暫悅後增苦 貪欲之想亦復然 始雖樂著終多患
见身实相皆不净 即是观于空无我 若能修习斯观者 于利益中最无上	見身實相皆不淨 即是觀於空無我 若能修習斯觀者 於利益中最無上
虽有色族及多闻 若无戒智犹禽兽 虽处丑贱少闻见 能修戒智名胜[1]士	雖有色族及多聞 若無戒智猶禽獸 雖處醜賤少聞見 能修戒智名勝[1]士

B. On the Hazards Inherent in Desire

18 (T23)

Desire is as devoid of beneficial aspects as an enemy or poison.
Such a declaration was uttered by the Muni himself.
Entrapment in cyclic birth-and-death is worse than being imprisoned.
Thus one should diligently cultivate the practices, seeking liberation.

C. On the Superior Valor in Controlling Desire

19 (T24)

The six sense bases become restive and run to their objective realms.
One should restrain them. One must not be negligent in this.
If one is able to restrain the sense faculties in this manner,
This is superior to a valiant general's crushing of a strong enemy.

D. On the Unloveliness of the Body

20 (T25)

This body's impurities flow forth from nine openings,
Doing so ceaselessly like rivers flowing out to the sea.
A thin skin hides this, providing the appearance of purity,
Just as when someone puts on necklaces for personal adornment.
The wise even then nonetheless distinguish clearly
And, realizing its deceptiveness, bring forth renunciation.

21 (T26)

As when one with an itching disease approaches flames for relief,[22]
Although there is an initial brief pleasure, suffering later increases.
So too it is with lust-ridden thoughts:
Though one is first blissfully attached, the end brings much trouble.[23]

10. In Praise of Contemplation-Based Insight, Wisdom, and Moral Virtue

22 (T27)

If one observes the body's true character, it is all seen as impure,[24]
Just then contemplate its emptiness and absence of a self.
If one is able to cultivate the practice of this contemplation,
Among all of the beneficial endeavors, this is the most superior.[25]

23 (T28)

Though one possesses fine physical form, noble birth, and learning,
If he is bereft of moral virtue and wisdom, he just like an animal.
Though one is homely, low-born, and of little learning or experience,
If able to embody moral virtue and wisdom, he is a superior person.

简体字	正體字
利衰八法莫能免 若有除断真无匹 诸有沙门婆罗门 父母妻子及眷属	利衰八法莫能免 若有除斷真無匹 諸有沙門婆羅門 父母妻子及眷屬
莫为彼意受其言 广造不善非法行 设为此等起诸过 未来大苦唯身受	莫為彼意受其言 廣造不善非法行 設為此等起諸過 未來大苦唯身受
夫造众恶不即报 非如刀剑交伤割 临终罪相始俱现 后入地狱婴诸苦	夫造眾惡不即報 非如刀劍交傷割 臨終罪相始俱現 後入地獄嬰諸苦
信戒施闻慧惭愧 如是七法名圣财 真实无比牟尼说 超越世间众珍宝 大王若集此胜财 不久亦[2]证道场果	信戒施聞慧慚愧 如是七法名聖財 真實無比牟尼說 超越世間眾珍寶 大王若集此勝財 不久亦[2]證道場果
博弈饮酤好琴瑟 懈怠憍逸及恶友 非时轻躁多动乱 如斯七法当远离	博弈飲酤好琴瑟 懈怠憍逸及惡友 非時輕躁多動亂 如斯(七)[六]法當遠離
知足第一胜诸财 如此之言世尊说 知足虽贫可名富 有财多欲是名贫 若丰财业增诸苦 如龙多首益酸毒	知足第一勝諸財 如此之言世尊說 知足雖貧可名富 有財多欲是名貧 若豐財業增諸苦 如龍多首益酸毒

11. ON AVOIDING THE EIGHT WORLDLY DHARMAS AND OFFENSES INSPIRED BY OTHERS
24 (T29-30)
No one is able to avoid the eight dharmas of gain, loss, and so forth.[26]
By eliminating [their influence], one becomes truly incomparable.
As for any śramaṇa or brahman,
One's father or mother, one's wife, children, or retinue—

25
Do not, influenced by their ideas or words,
Commit any extensively unwholesome, Dharma-contravening deeds.
If you generate any sort of transgression on behalf of these or others,
You alone must endure the immense future suffering this entails.

12. ON THE DELAYED ARRIVAL OF KARMIC RETRIBUTIONS
26 (T31)
Now, doing many evil deeds does not bring immediate retribution.
It is not like crossing swords and thereupon receiving injurious cuts.
Only starting at the point of death are signs of retribution revealed.
Afterward, one falls into the hells and is then assailed by sufferings.

13. ON THE ĀRYAS' SEVEN FORMS OF WEALTH
27 (T32)
Faith, morality, giving, learning, wisdom, shame, dread of blame—
These seven dharmas are "the wealth of the Āryas."
The Muni declared them to be genuine and incomparable,
Far surpassing the many precious jewels found in the world.
Great King, if one accumulates these superior forms of wealth,
He too may before long realize the fruits of the *bodhimaṇḍala*.[27]

14. ON SIX COARSE FAULTS TO BE ELIMINATED
28 (T33)
Gambling, inebriation, fondness for musical entertainments,
Unrestrained indulgence in indolence, consorting with bad friends,
And rousting about creating disturbances at inappropriate times—
These six dharmas should be abandoned.[28]

15. IN PRAISE OF BEING EASILY SATISFIED
29 (T34-5)
Being easily satisfied is the most supreme of all forms of wealth.
Words of this sort were uttered by the Bhagavān.
When easily satisfied, though poor, one still qualifies as wealthy.
When rich, if one has many desires, this still amounts to poverty.
If one lives the life of abundant wealth, this increases one's sufferings,
Just as a many-headed dragon suffers an increased amount of pain.[29]

简体字	正體字
当观美味如毒药 以智慧水灑令净 为存此身虽应食 勿贪色味长憍慢	當觀美味如毒藥 以智慧水灑令淨 為存此身雖應食 勿貪色味長憍慢
于诸欲染当生厌 勤求无上涅盘道 调和此身令安隐 然后宜应修斋戒	於諸欲染當生厭 勤求無上涅槃道 調和此身令安隱 然後宜應修齋戒
一夜分别有五时 于[3]二时中当眠息 初中后夜观生死 宜勤求度勿空过	一夜分別有五時 於[3]二時中當眠息 初中後夜觀生死 宜勤求度勿空過
四无量定当修习 是名开于梵天道 若专系念四禅心 命终必生彼天处	四無量定當修習 是名開於梵天道 若專繫念四禪心 命終必生彼天處
有为迁动皆无常 苦空败坏不坚固 无我无乐不清净 如是悉名对治法	有為遷動皆無常 苦空敗壞不堅固 無我無樂不清淨 如是悉名對治法
若有深观此法门 未来常处尊豪位 修行五戒断五邪 是亦大王所应念	若有深觀此法門 未來常處尊豪位 修行五戒斷五邪 是亦大王所應念

16. On Moderation and Sensibility in Eating
30 (T38)
One should contemplate even exquisite flavors as like toxic medicines
On which one sprinkles the waters of wisdom to make them pure.
Although one should eat for the sake of insuring survival of this body,
Do not crave food's form or flavor or let it lead to pretentiousness.

17. Renounce Desires, Seek Nirvāṇa, Regulate the Body, Take up the Upavāsa
31 (TX)
One should generate renunciation for the defilement of the desires
And should diligently seek the unsurpassed path to nirvāṇa.
One should train and regulate this body in a way securing its welfare.
Afterwards, it is fitting to cultivate the abstinence rite precepts.[30]

18. Exhortation to Encourage Diligence in cultivating the Path
32 (T39)
A single night is divided into five periods.[31]
In two of them, one should allow oneself to sleep.
Contemplate birth-and-death at night's beginning, middle, and end.
Diligence in seeking liberation is fitting. Do not let time pass emptily.

19. On the Four Immeasurable Minds and Cultivation of Dhyāna Absorptions
33 (T40-1)
One should cultivate the four immeasurables' meditative absorptions.
These are renowned for opening the path to the Brahma Heavens.[32]
If one focuses mindfulness on the four dhyānas' mind-states,
At life's end, one will certainly be reborn in those celestial abodes.[33]

20. On the Necessity of Cultivating Counteractive Dharmas
34 (T42)
All which transpires in conditioned existence is impermanent,
Suffering, empty of inherent existence, destructible, nondurable,
Devoid of self, devoid of bliss, and impure.
[Contemplations of] all such concepts serve as counteractive dharmas.

35
If one develops deep contemplations on these gateways to Dharma,
In the future, he will always abide in esteemed and powerful stations.
As for five-precepts practice and severance of those five wrong deeds,
The Great King should be all the more mindful of these.

简体字	正體字
譬如少盐置恒河 不能令水有醎味 微细之恶遇众善 消灭散坏亦如是	譬如少鹽置恒河 不能令水有醎味 微細之惡遇眾善 消滅散壞亦如是
五邪若增劫功德 王当除灭令莫长 信等五根众善源 是宜修习令增[4]盛	五邪若增劫功德 王當除滅令莫長 信等五根眾善源 是宜修習令增[4]盛
生等八苦常炽燃 [5]当持慧水灑令灭 欲求天乐及涅盘 应勤修习正知见	生等八苦常熾燃 [5]當持慧水灑令滅 欲求天樂及涅槃 應勤修習正知見
虽有利智入邪道 微妙功德永无馀 四种颠倒害诸善 是故当观莫令生	雖有利智入邪道 微妙功德永無餘 四種顛倒害諸善 是故當觀莫令生
谓色非我我非色 我中无色色无我 于色生此四种心 自馀诸阴皆如是 是二十心名颠倒 若能除断为最上	謂色非我我非色 我中無色色無我 於色生此四種心 自餘諸陰皆如是 是二十心名顛倒 若能除斷為最上
法不自起冥初生 非自在作及时有 皆从无明爱业起 若无因缘便断坏 大王既知此等因 当燃慧灯破痴暗	法不自起冥初生 非自在作及時有 皆從無明愛業起 若無因緣便斷壞 大王既知此等因 當燃慧燈破癡闇

21. On the Mitigating Effect of Predominant Goodness

36 (T43)

Just as a little salt placed in the Ganges River
Is unable to make its waters salty,
So too, when minor evil encounters abundant goodness,
Its dispersion and dilution is much the same.

22. Five Wrong Actions as Thieves; Five Root-Faculties as Sources of Goodness

37 (T44-5)

If the five erroneous deeds increase, they steal away one's merit.[34]
The King should do away with them, preventing them from growing.
The five root-faculties of faith and such are sources of much good.[35]
It is these one should cultivate and allow to develop abundantly.

23. Suffering, Its Origin, and Necessity of Right Views to Liberation

A. The Eight Sufferings; The Necessity of Right Views

38 (T46-7)

The eight sufferings of birth and such are constant in their blazing.[36]
With the waters of wisdom, one should douse and extinguish them.
Whether one desires to strive for heavenly bliss or for nirvāṇa,
One must diligently cultivate right knowledge and views.

B. The Four Inverted Views and the Harm They Wreak

39 (T48)

Though possessing sharp intelligence, if one enters erroneous paths,
One's sublime qualities will disappear forever and leave not a trace.
The four types of inverted views do harm to every form of goodness.
Therefore, one must contemplate them and prevent their arising.

C. Right and Wrong Views on the Aggregates

1. The Nonexistence of Any "Self" Associated with the Five Aggregates

40 (T49)

[The Buddha] has declared that form is not self, self is not form,
There is no form in a self, and there is no self in form.
These four ideas are conceived in relation to the form aggregate.
Any link of a "self" to the other aggregates is in all respects the same.
These twenty ideas are inverted views.
If one can cut them off entirely, this is the most superior [insight].

2. On the Origins of the Aggregates

41 (T50)

Those dharmas arose neither spontaneously nor primordially,
Were not created by the Iśvara god, and were not created by time.
They have all arisen through ignorance, craving, and karmic action.
Absent any specific cause or condition, they are then destroyed.
Great King, having realized the nature of such causes,
One should light wisdom's lamp to dispel darkness of ignorance.[37]

简体字	正體字
身见戒取及疑结 此三能障无漏道 王若毁坏令散灭 圣解脱法当现显	身見戒取及疑結 此三能障無漏道 王若毀壞令散滅 聖解脫法當現顯
譬如盲人问水相 百千万劫莫[6]能了 欲求涅盘亦如是 唯自精勤后方证	譬如盲人問水相 百千萬劫莫[6]能了 欲求涅槃亦如是 唯自精勤後方證
欲假眷属及知识 而得之者甚难[7]有 是故大王当[8]精进 然后乃可证寂灭	欲假眷屬及知識 而得之者甚難[7]有 是故大王當[8]精進 然後乃可證寂滅
施戒多闻及禅定 因是渐近四真谛 人主故应修慧明 行斯三法求解脱 若能修此最上乘 则摄诸馀一切善	施戒多聞及禪定 因是漸近四真諦 人主故應修慧明 行斯三法求解脫 若能修此最上乘 則攝諸餘一切善
大王当观身念[9]法 世尊说为清净道 若无此念增恶觉 是故宜应勤修习	大王當觀身念[9]法 世尊說為清淨道 若無此念增惡覺 是故宜應勤修習
人命短促不久留 如水上泡起寻灭 出息入息眠睡间 念念恒谢常衰[10]灭	人命短促不久留 如水上泡起尋滅 出息入息眠睡間 念念恒謝常衰[10]滅

D. Three Fetters Impeding Liberation
42 (T51)
Viewing body as self, clinging to prohibitions, the fetter of doubt—
These three can block the path to freedom from outflow impurities.
If the King destroys them, thus causing them to disappear,
The Āryas' dharma of liberation will then manifest.

24. The Necessity to Liberation of Self-Reliance
43 (T52)
As when blind men inquire about the appearance of bodies of water,
But in a hundred thousand myriad kalpas can never comprehend it,
So too it is with the striving for nirvāṇa.
That realization is gained only after one's own diligent efforts.

44
If one wished to rely upon one's retinue or advisors
As means to gain it, this would be extremely difficult to bring about.
Therefore the Great King should take up the practice vigorously.
Then he will subsequently be able to realize quiescent cessation.

25. The Three Trainings: Moral Virtue; Dhyāna Concentration; Wisdom
45 (T53)
Implement moral virtue, much learning, and dhyāna concentration.
Through these, one gradually draws close to the four truths.
The ruler among men should therefore cultivate wisdom's clarity
And practice these three dharmas through which to seek liberation.
If one is able to cultivate this most supreme of vehicles,
Then one will thereby subsume all other forms of goodness.

26. The Station of Mindfulness with Respect to the Body
46 (T54)
The Great King should contemplate the body-mindfulness dharmas.
The Bhagavān described them as the path to purification.
If one is without this mindfulness, one increases unwholesome ideas.
Therefore it is only fitting that one should diligently cultivate this.

47 (T55)
This human life is brief, hurried, and not retained for long.
It is like a water bubble which, once arisen, is straightaway destroyed.
Even as one exhales and then inhales, and even during sleep,
In each instant, it constantly retreats, always going toward ruination.

简体字	正體字
不久便当见磨灭 皮肉臭烂甚可恶 青瘀胀坏脓血流 虫蛆唼食至枯竭 发毛爪齿各分散 风吹日曝渐[11]乾尽	不久便當見磨滅 皮肉臭爛甚可惡 青瘀脹壞膿血流 虫蛆唼食至枯竭 髮毛爪齒各分散 風吹日曝漸[11]乾盡
当知此身不坚牢 无量众苦所积聚 是故贤圣诸智人 皆观斯过咸弃舍	當知此身不堅牢 無量眾苦所積聚 是故賢聖諸智人 皆觀斯過咸棄捨
须弥巨海及江河 七日并照皆融竭 如此坚固尚摧毁 况复若斯危脆身	須彌巨海及江河 七日並照皆融竭 如此堅固尚摧毀 況復若斯危脆身
无常既至无救护 不可恃怙及追求 是故大王[12]常谛观 速生厌离求胜法	無常既至無救護 不可恃怙及追求 是故大王[12]常諦觀 速生厭離求勝法
人身难得法难闻 犹如盲龟遇浮孔 既获若斯希有身 宜应勤心听正法	人身難得法難聞 猶如盲龜遇浮孔 既獲若斯希有身 宜應勤心聽正法
得此妙身造诸恶 譬如宝器盛众毒 生处中国遇善友 专念发心起正愿	得此妙身造諸惡 譬如寶器盛眾毒 生處中國遇善友 專念發心起正願
久殖功德具诸根 王今满足此众善 若复亲近[13]见知人 佛说此为净梵行	久殖功德具諸根 王今滿足此眾善 若復親近[13]見知人 佛說此為淨梵行

48 (T56)
It will not be long before it will be worn down and destroyed,
Whereupon skin and flesh smell, rot, and turn extremely loathsome.
It turns stagnant-blood blue, bloats, fissures, and spills pus and blood.
It is eaten at by worms until it becomes withered and dried up.
The body and head hair, nails and teeth each separate and scatter.
Blown by wind, baked by sun, it slowly dries and disappears entirely.

49
One should realize that this body is not solid or durable.
It is the place where the many forms of suffering assemble together.
Therefore the Worthies, the Āryas, and all wise people
Contemplate these faults and thus are moved to renounce it.

50 (T57)
Mount Sumeru, the great seas, and the rivers as well
Will all be melted and dried up when the seven suns shine all at once.
If even such durable phenomena as those are utterly destroyed,
How much the more must that be true of this ever so fragile body?

51 (T58)
Once impermanence arrives, one is beyond rescue or protection.
It cannot be relied upon nor can one find any means of escape in it.
Therefore the Great King should always and truly contemplate this,
Swiftly generate renunciation, and seek out the supreme Dharma.

52 (T59)
The human body is so rarely gained and the Dharma so rarely heard
That meeting them is as rare as a blind turtle's head happening to
    poke up into a floating wooden yoke.[38]
Having obtained a human body in such rare circumstances as these,
It is only right that one diligently obey the dictates of right Dharma.

53 (T60-1)
To gain this marvelous body and yet commit all manner of evil deeds
Is analogous to filling up a jeweled vessel with all sorts of poison.
Having been born in a central land and met a good spiritual friend,[39]
One should focus the mind, generate resolve, and initiate right vows.

27. ON THE CIRCUMSTANCES REQUISITE FOR CULTIVATING THE PATH

54 (T62)
Through long sowing merit and equipping himself with the faculties,
The King is now able to completely fulfill these many forms of good.
If one is also able to draw close to a man of vision and knowledge—
The Buddha declared that this is the basis of pure brahmin conduct.

简体字	正體字
是故应当乐随顺 诸佛由此证涅盘 既遇微妙清净法 应当志求离欲道	是故應當樂隨順 諸佛由此證涅槃 既遇微妙清淨法 應當志求離欲道
生死崄难苦无量 穷劫宣说莫能尽 我今为王略分别 应当谛听善思惟	生死崄難苦無量 窮劫宣說莫能盡 我今為王略分別 應當諦聽善思惟
三界转变无轮际 父母妻子更相因 怨亲[14]憎爱无常处 如旋火轮岂穷已	三界轉變無輪際 父母妻子更相因 怨親[14]憎愛無常處 如旋火輪豈窮已
无始生死世界来 计饮母乳多大海 若不精勤证空智 将来复饮无穷限	無始生死世界來 計飲母乳多大海 若不精勤證空智 將來復飲無窮限
周流五道经人天 若积身骨高须弥 爱别哀悲计其泪 亦非江河所能匹	周流五道經人天 若積身骨高須彌 愛別哀悲計其淚 亦非江河所能匹
若计一人父母者 过于世间草木数 虽受五欲天上乐 终还坠没恶趣苦	若計一人父母者 過於世間草木數 雖受五欲天上樂 終還墜沒惡趣苦
诸天寿命极长远 其间娱乐难宣说 歌讴倡舞流妙声 哀音和雅甚清远	諸天壽命極長遠 其間娛樂難宣說 歌謳倡舞流妙聲 哀音和雅甚清遠

55
One should therefore find happiness in according with this.
It is on account of this that all Buddhas gained realization of nirvāṇa.
Having encountered this sublime and pure Dharma,
One should resolutely seek out the path abandoning desire.

28. Description of the Faults of Cyclic Existence
A. An Introductory General Description of Faults

56 (T65)
Birth and death's perilous hardships and woes are so innumerable
That, expound on them for a kalpa, none could utterly describe them.
As I now briefly distinguish them for the benefit of the King,
He should listen carefully and reflect upon them well.

57 (T66)
There is no end to the three realms' cycle of transformations where[40]
Fathers, mothers, wives, and children alternate in causal relations.
Hatred or loving between enemies or kin have no lasting bases.[41]
As with the twirling firebrand's "wheel," how could this cycle end?[42]

58 (T67)
Through worldly existences in beginningless births and deaths,
The mothers' milk consumed is greater than the great sea's waters.
If one fails to be intensely diligent realizing emptiness and wisdom,
One will consume endlessly more in the course of one's future lives.

59 (T68)
Flowing throughout five destinies and in lives as humans and gods—
Piling up those bodies' bones, their height rivals even Mount Sumeru.
As for tears shed weeping in grief over separation from those loved,
Not even the great rivers' waters are adequate to provide comparison.

60 (T70)
Were one to count up the number of one person's fathers and mothers,
They would surpass the number of grasses and trees in the world.
Though one may enjoy celestial bliss amidst the heaven's five desires,
One finally falls back down, sinking in the wretched destinies' pains.

B. The Gods
61
The lifespans of the gods extending extremely far into the future.
The sensual bliss they experience would be difficult even to describe.
Their singing and dances stream forth sublime sounds.
The plaintive voices are harmonious, intensely clear, and far-reaching.

奇姿妙色极端严 围遶侍卫相娱乐 百味盛馔皆具足 随意所歆自然至	奇姿妙色極端嚴 圍遶侍衛相娛樂 百味盛饌皆具足 隨意所歆自然至
宝池香净水恒满 周匝罗覆诸妙花 众鸟异色集其上 哀声相和出远音	寶池香淨水恒滿 周匝羅覆諸妙花 眾鳥異色集其上 哀聲相和出遠音
诸天游戏浴其内 如是欢娱不可说 福尽临终五衰现 尔时[1]生苦逾前乐	諸天遊戲浴其內 如是歡娛不可說 福盡臨終五衰現 爾時[1]生苦踰前樂
是故虽有天女娱 智者见之已生厌 虽居珍宝上楼观 亦必退堕臭秽处	是故雖有天女娛 智者見之已生厭 雖居珍寶上樓觀 亦必退墮臭穢處
虽游天上难陀园 会亦还入刀剑林 虽浴诸天曼陀池 终必坠于灰河狱	雖遊天上難陀園 會亦還入刀劍林 雖浴諸天曼陀池 終必墜於灰河獄
虽复位处转轮帝 归为僮仆被驱[2]使 虽受梵天离欲娱 还坠无间炽然苦	雖復位處轉輪帝 歸為僮僕被驅[2]使 雖受梵天離欲娛 還墜無間熾然苦
虽居天宫具光明 后入地狱黑暗中 所谓黑绳活[3]地狱 烧割剥刺及无间	雖居天宮具光明 後入地獄黑闇中 所謂黑繩活[3]地獄 燒割剝刺及無間

简体字　　　　　　　　　　正體字

62
Those of rare charms, sublime physical form, and graceful adornment
Surround and wait on one, engaging him in the sensual pleasures.
Fine cuisine replete with a hundred flavors is all abundantly present.
Whatever one wishes for in amusement spontaneously arrives.

63
Bejeweled bathing pools, always brimming with fragrant pure water,
Are ringed and overhung with all varieties of marvelous blossoms.
A multitude of birds in exotic colors flock together just above,
Their rarefied sounds harmonious, send forth distantly-ranging calls.

C. On the Unpredictability of Ostensibly Desirable States of Existence

64
The gods roam about, sporting playfully, bathing themselves therein.
Such joys and sensual blisses cannot even be described.
As merit runs out, they come to the end, and five signs of ruin appear.
They are then beset by suffering exceeding their earlier pleasures.[43]

65 (T71)
Thus, though one may enjoy the sensual pleasure of celestial maidens,
As the wise behold them, they have already generated renunciation.
Although one may abide atop a jewel-encrusted viewing tower.
Still, he will certainly plummet back down and abide in stinking filth.

66 (T72-3)
Though one may roam up to the heavens into the Garden of Nanda,
One will still return again to enter the Sword-Tree Forest Hells.
Although one might bathe in the *mandārava* blossom pools of the gods,
In the end, one surely plummets into the molten River-of-Ashes Hells.

67 (T69, 74)
Although one might reign again as a wheel-turning monarch,
He will return thereafter to become a slave ordered about by others.
Though one may enjoy desire-transcending bliss in brahma heavens,
He will fall back into the pain of the Non-Intermittent Hells' flames.[44]

D. The Hells

68 (T75, 77)
Even if one abides in celestial palaces resplendent with brilliant light,
He will afterwards enter into the darkness of the hells,
Namely the Black-Line Hells and Living Hells, where he is
Burnt, cut, skinned, and impaled, and also the Non-Intermittent Hell.

是八地狱常炽燃 皆是众生恶业报 [4]或受大苦如[5]押油 或碎身体若尘粉	是八地獄常熾燃 皆是眾生惡業報 [4]或受大苦如[5]押油 或碎身體若塵粉
或解[6]支节[7]今分散 或复[利-禾+皮]剥及烧煮 或以沸铜澍其口 或以铁[*]押裂其形	或解[6]支節[7]今[令]分散 或復[利-禾+皮]剝及燒煮 或以沸銅澍其口 或以鐵[*]押裂其形
铁狗竞来争食噉 铁[8]鸟复集共[9]齟掣 众类毒虫并[齿*齐]齧 或烧铜柱贯其身	鐵狗競來爭食噉 鐵[8]鳥復集共[9]齟掣 眾類毒虫並[齒*齊]齧 或燒銅柱貫其身
大火猛盛俱洞燃 罪业缘故无逃避 钁汤腾沸至高涌 颠倒罪人投其内	大火猛盛俱洞燃 罪業緣故無逃避 鑊湯騰沸至高涌 顛倒罪人投其內
人命危朽甚迅驶 譬如诸天喘息顷 若人于此短命中 闻上诸苦不惊畏 当知此心甚坚固 犹如金刚难摧坏	人命危朽甚迅駛 譬如諸天喘息頃 若人於此短命中 聞上諸苦不驚畏 當知此心甚堅固 猶如金剛難摧壞
若见图画闻他言 或随经书自忆念 如是知时[10]已难忍 况复己身自经历	若見圖畫聞他言 或隨經書自憶念 如是知時[10]已難忍 況復己身自經歷
无间无救大地狱 此中诸苦难穷尽 若复有人一日中以三百[11] 鉾[打-丁+(臾-火+焱)]其体	無間無救大地獄 此中諸苦難窮盡 若復有人一日中以三百[11] 鉾[打-丁+(臾-火+焱)]其體
简体字	正體字

69 (T78)
These eight types of hells are constant in their burning
And in every case exist as retribution for the evil karma of beings.
One may endure there such great sufferings as that of the "oil-press,"
Or that of the body's being ground up as fine as motes of dust.

70 (T79)
One may have the limbs cut off so that they become scattered,[45]
One may be skinned and roasted,
One may have boiling molten copper poured down one's gullet,
Or one may have his body split open by an iron press.

71 (T80)
Iron dogs rush forth, struggling with each other to devour one's flesh.
Iron birds swarm down in flocks, all striking at once with their beaks.
Many sorts of poisonous insects chew away at one's flesh.
Or one is burnt by a brass pillar impaling the body's entire length.

72 (T82)
A huge blaze, fierce and full, blazes intensely everywhere.
As this is caused by offense karma, one cannot run away or avoid it.
The pot's broth splashes up as it boils, leaping to the highest heights.
Then those with inverted-view karmic offenses are heaved on into it.

73 (T83)
The human life is vulnerable to ruin, extremely swift in its passing,
And comparable in length to but a single breath of a god.
If a person in the midst of this brief life
Hears of the sufferings described above but is not terrified by them,
One should realize this sort of mind is so extreme in its obduracy
As to be comparable to *vajra* in the difficulty of breaking it open.

74 (T84)
If one views illustrations of them, hears someone else describe them,
Or reflects upon them in accordance with the scriptural descriptions,
Then, having become aware of them, one finds them difficult to bear.
How much the more so were one bound to undergo them himself.

75 (T86)
In the non-intermittent, inescapable great hells,
The sufferings endured would be difficult to exhaustively describe.
If there was a person who in the course of a single day
Was compelled to endure three hundred spears assailing his body,

比阿[12]毘獄一念苦 百千万分不及一 受此大苦经一劫 罪业缘尽后方免 如是苦恼从谁生 皆由三业不善起 大王今虽无斯患 若不修因[13]缘[14]坠落 于畜生中苦无量 或有系缚及鞭挞 无有信戒多闻故 恒怀恶心相食噉 或为明珠羽角牙 骨毛皮肉致残害 为人乘驾不自在 恒受瓦石刀杖苦 饿鬼道中苦亦然 诸所须欲不随意 饥渴所逼[15]困寒热 疲乏等苦甚无量 腹大若山咽如针 [16]屎尿脓血不可说 裸形被发甚丑恶 如多罗树被烧剪 其口夜则大火燃 诸虫争赴共唼食 屎尿粪秽诸不净 百千万劫莫能得 设复推求得少分 更相劫夺寻散失	比阿[12]毘獄一念苦 百千萬分不及一 受此大苦經一劫 罪業緣盡後方免 如是苦惱從誰生 皆由三業不善起 大王今雖無斯患 若不修因[13]緣[14]墜落 於畜生中苦無量 或有繫縛及鞭撻 無有信戒多聞故 恒懷惡心相食噉 或為明珠羽角牙 骨毛皮肉致殘害 為人乘駕不自在 恒受瓦石刀杖苦 餓鬼道中苦亦然 諸所須欲不隨意 飢渴所逼[15]困寒熱 疲乏等苦甚無量 腹大若山咽如針 [16]屎尿膿血不可說 裸形被髮甚醜惡 如多羅樹被燒剪 其口夜則大火燃 諸虫爭赴共唼食 屎尿糞穢諸不淨 百千萬劫莫能得 設復推求得少分 更相劫奪尋散失
简体字	正體字

76 (T87)
Compared to a single instant of the suffering in the Avīci Hells,
It would not even come close to equaling a billionth part.
One undergoes this great suffering, passing through an entire kalpa.
Only after offense karma has been exhausted is one able to escape it.

77 (T88)
By who are such sufferings as these produced?
They all arise through unskillful generation of three types of karma.
Great King, although one is now free of these sorts of troubles,
If one fails to cultivate causes and conditions, he will fall down below.

E. The Animals
78 (T89)
The suffering within the realm of animals is incalculably great.
They are subjected therein to being bound up, whipped, or beaten.
Due to having no faith, moral virtue, or learning,
They constantly cherish evil thoughts and devour one another.

79 (T90)
It may be that, due to quests for bright pearls, feathers, horns, tusks,
Bones, fur, hides, or flesh, one is subjected to excruciating injury.
One may be ridden by people, deprived of independence,
And constantly endure suffering from tiles, stones, knives, or staves.

F. The Hungry Ghosts
80 (T91)
The suffering endured in the hungry ghost realm is of the same sort.
Whatever they need or desire does not come in accord with wishes.
They are driven by hunger and thirst and straitened by cold and heat.
Pains such as weariness and privation are extreme and incalculable.

81 (T92-3)
Their bellies are the size of mountains and their throats like needles.
Their seeking for feces, urine, pus, and blood is unspeakably horrible.
They go naked, are robed in hair, and are very ugly and loathsome,
Appearing like *tāla* trees burned and damaged by hacking.
At night, their mouths blaze with a great fire
Causing insects to struggle to fly in where they are eaten as food.

82 (T94)
Though they seek excrement's fecal filth, urine, and other impurities,
They are still unable to obtain them as food even in a billion kalpas.
If it happens while seeking them, they obtain even a small portion,
They steal it away from each other so that it is soon scattered and lost.

清[17]凉秋月患焰热
温和春日转寒苦
若趣园林众果尽
设至清流变枯[18]竭

罪业缘故寿长远
经有一万五千岁
受众楚毒无空缺
皆是饿鬼之果报
正觉说斯苦恼因
名曰悭贪嫉妒业

若天福尽有馀善
因此得为人中王
后设懈怠福都尽
必坠三恶无有疑

或生修罗起贡高
恚嫉贪害增诸恼
诸天虽有善根行
以其悭嫉失利乐
是故当知嫉妒结
为[19]深恶法宜弃舍

大王汝今已[20]具知
生死过[21]患多众苦
应当勤修出世善
如渴思饮救头燃
若加精进断诸有
于诸善中最无上

简体字

清[17]涼秋月患焰熱
溫和春日轉寒苦
若趣園林眾果盡
設至清流變枯[18]竭

罪業緣故壽長遠
經有一萬五千歲
受眾楚毒無空缺
皆是餓鬼之果報
正覺說斯苦惱因
名曰慳貪嫉妒業

若天福盡有餘善
因此得為人中王
後設懈怠福都盡
必墜三惡無有疑

或生修羅起貢高
恚嫉貪害增諸惱
諸天雖有善根行
以其慳嫉失利樂
是故當知嫉妒結
為[19]深惡法宜棄捨

大王汝今已[20]具知
生死過[21]患多眾苦
應當勤修出世善
如渴思飲救頭燃
若加精進斷諸有
於諸善中最無上

正體字

83 (T95)
The clear and cool autumn moon afflicts them with flaming heat.
The warm, agreeable spring sun turns into intense cold's suffering.
If they go into an orchard, the many fruits all disappear.
On reaching clear flowing water, it transforms and entirely dries up.

84 (T96-7)
Due to the karmic offenses they have committed, their lives last long,
Going on even for a period of fifteen thousand years.
They endure without respite many sorts of excruciating sufferings,
All of these are forms of karmic retribution visited on hungry ghosts.
The Rightly Enlightened One described such bitter afflictions' causes,
Declaring them to be the karma of miserly covetousness and jealousy.

G. Rebirth Scenarios of the Gods
85 (T101)
If one's god-realm merit is ended, but good causes still remain,
He may yet succeed in becoming a king within the human realm.
If one then indulges indolence, his merit becomes entirely exhausted
And, without a doubt, he plummets into the three wretched destinies.

H. The Asuras
86 (T102)
One may be reborn among *asuras* and thus become arrogant,
Hateful, jealous, covetous, harmful, and bound to increase afflictions.
Though the gods coursed in actions producing roots of goodness,
Here, due to stinginess and jealously, one loses such benefits' bliss.[46]
Therefore one should realize that the fetter of jealousy
Amounts to a profoundly evil dharma fit to be cast out.

I. Summation on Cyclic Existence with Exhortation to Pursue the Path
87 (T103-4)
Great King, you now already completely realize
The faults, troubles, and many sufferings in cyclic births and deaths.
You should cultivate world-transcending goodness with urgency,
As one seeks water when thirsty or douses a turban that's caught fire.
If one is vigorous in severing one's coursing in all realms of existence,
This, among all forms of goodness, is the sort most unsurpassed.

简体字	正體字
当勤持戒习禅智 调伏其心求涅盘 涅盘微妙绝诸相 无生老死及衰恼 亦无山河与日月 是故应当速证知	當勤持戒習禪智 調伏其心求涅槃 涅槃微妙絕諸相 無生老死及衰惱 亦無山河與日月 是故應當速證知
若欲证于无师智 应当专修七觉法 若有乘斯觉分船 生死大海易超渡	若欲證於無師智 應當專修七覺法 若有乘斯覺分船 生死大海易超渡
佛所不说十四法 但生信心莫疑惑 唯当正心勤精进 决定修习诸善法	佛所不說十四法 但生信心莫疑惑 唯當正心勤精進 決定修習諸善法
无明缘行识名色 六入触受爱取有 有则缘生生缘死 若尽生死因缘灭	無明緣行識名色 六入觸受愛取有 有則緣生生緣死 若盡生死因緣滅
如是正观十二缘 是人则见圣师子 若欲次第见四谛 当勤修习八正道	如是正觀十二緣 是人則見聖師子 若欲次第見四諦 當勤修習八正道
虽居尊荣处五欲 亦得圣道断诸结 此果不可求馀人 必自心会乃得证	雖居尊榮處五欲 亦得聖道斷諸結 此果不可求餘人 必自心會乃得證

29. Encouragement to Cultivate the Three Trainings and Seek Nirvāṇa
88 (T105)
Be diligent in moral precepts, practicing dhyāna, and wisdom,
Thus training the mind and striving toward nirvāṇa.
Nirvāṇa is sublime, transcends all signs,
Is free of birth, aging, death, and afflictions wrought by destruction,
And is even devoid of mountains and rivers, sun and moon.
One should therefore be swift in achieving its realization.

30. The Seven Limbs of Enlightenment
89 (T106)
If one wishes to realize the wisdom not dependent on any guru,
One should focus on cultivating the seven enlightenment dharmas.[47]
If one boards this ship of the limbs of enlightenment,
It will become easy to cross beyond the great sea of births and deaths.

31. Avoidance of the Fourteen Indeterminate Dharmas
90 (T108)
As for those fourteen dharmas the Buddha declined to discuss,[48]
Simply have faith, refraining from doubts and delusions.
One should devote oneself solely to right-minded diligence and vigor,
Remaining resolutely determined to cultivate all good dharmas.

32. The Twelve-Fold Causal Chain, the Four Truths, and the Eightfold Path
91 (T109-11)
Ignorance conditions karmic action, consciousness, name-and-form,
Six sense bases, contact, feeling, craving, grasping, and becoming.[49]
Becoming then conditions birth and birth conditions death.
If one ends one's births, the causes and conditions for death cease.

92 (T112-4)
If there be someone who rightly contemplates these twelve conditions,
Then he will thereby behold the Lion of the Āryas.[50]
If one wishes to succeed in sequential perception of the four truths,[51]
He should diligently cultivate the eight-fold right path.[52]

III. Concluding Exhortatory Section
93 (T115)
Although one might abide in honor and glory amidst the five desires,
One may still realizing the path of the Āryas by severing the fetters.
This sort of fruition is not such as one might seek from others.
One must embody it in his own mind to succeed in its realization.

简体字	正體字
我说众苦及涅盘 欲为润益大王故 不应生于怖畏心 但勤诵习行诸善	我說眾苦及涅槃 欲為潤益大王故 不應生於怖畏心 但勤誦習行諸善
心为诸法之根本 若先调伏事斯办 我说法要略分别 王不宜应生足心	心為諸法之根本 若先調伏事斯辦 我說法要略分別 王不宜應生足心
若有大智更敷演 亦当至心勤听受 王今名为大法器 若广闻法必多益	若有大智更敷演 亦當至心勤聽受 王今名為大法器 若廣聞法必多益
若见有修三业善 应深助生随喜心 自所行善及随喜 如是功德悉迴向	若見有修三業善 應深助生隨喜心 自所行善及隨喜 如是功德悉迴向
王当仰学诸贤圣 如观音等度众生 未来必当成正觉 国无生老三毒害	王當仰學諸賢聖 如觀音等度眾生 未來必當成正覺 國無生老三毒害
大王若修上诸善 则美名称广流布 然后以此教化人 普令一切成正觉	大王若修上諸善 則美名稱廣流布 然後以此教化人 普令一切成正覺
烦恼驶河[22][漂*寸]众生 为深怖畏炽然苦 欲灭如是诸尘劳 应修真实解脱谛 离诸世间假名法 则得清净不动处	煩惱駛河[22][漂*寸]眾生 為深怖畏熾然苦 欲滅如是諸塵勞 應修真實解脫諦 離諸世間假名法 則得清淨不動處

94 (T117)
I have explained the manifold sufferings as well as nirvāṇa
Out of a wish to be of benefit to the Great King.
You should not allow your mind to succumb to fearfulness.
Simply recite and practice this diligently, devoting yourself to good.

95
The mind is the root of all dharmas.
If one first trains and subdues it, one's endeavors thereby succeed.
In discussing Dharma's essentials, I give only a general explanation.
Thus it would not be fitting for the King to be satisfied merely by this.

96
For the immensely wise, one would expound more extensively.
Still, one should listen and absorb this with an utterly sincere mind.
The King now qualifies as a great vessel for the retention of Dharma.
If one has vast Dharma learning, one certainly provides much benefit.

97 (T119)
On observing someone cultivating goodness in the three karmas,
One should be profoundly helpful and feel concordant joy in it.[53]
One should dedicate [to highest enlightenment] all of the merit
From one's own practice of goodness and from concordant rejoicing.

98 (T120)
The King should look up in his studies to the Worthies and the Āryas
And strive to liberate beings just as do Avalokiteśvara and the others.
In the future, you will certainly be able to realize right enlightenment
In a land free of cyclic birth, aging, and harm from the three poisons.

99
If the Great King cultivates all of the superior forms of goodness,
Then a fine reputation will circulate widely.
He may thereafter employ these teachings in the instruction of others
And influence everyone toward realization of right enlightenment.

100
The bounding floods of the torrents of afflictions inundate beings,
Deeply terrorizing them and subjecting them to burning sufferings.[54]
If one wishes to extinguish such sense-object weariness as this,
One must cultivate the truths leading to genuine liberation.
If one abandons the dharmas of the world's false naming,
Then one will gain the station of purity and immovability.

若有妇人怀害心 如此之妻宜远离 设有贞和爱敬夫 谦卑勤业若婢使 恒为亲友姊母想 此宜尊敬如宅神 我所说法正如是 王当日夜勤修行 龙树菩萨 为禅陀迦王说法要偈	若有婦人懷害心 如此之妻宜遠離 設有貞和愛敬夫 謙卑勤業若婢使 恒為親友姊母想 此宜尊敬如宅神 我所說法正如是 王當日夜勤修行 龍樹菩薩 為禪陀迦王說法要偈
简体字	正體字

01. ADDENDUM ON THE VARIOUS SORTS OF CANDIDATES FOR MARRIAGE
101   (T36-7)
Were one to consider as a wife someone cherishing thoughts of harm,
It would only be right to avoid such a mate.
If one were to have a chaste, harmonious, loving, and respectful mate
As humbly deferential and diligent in endeavors as a maidservant,
Or one who always acts like a close friend, a sister, or a mother,
It would be fitting to honor and respect her like a household deity.

02. FINAL CLOSING STATEMENT
102
The Dharma which I proclaim is of this very sort.
The King should be dedicated day and night to its diligent cultivation.

The Dharma Essentials Verses
Composed by Nāgārjuna Bodhisattva for King Śatakarṇī

(The end of the Tripiṭaka Master Guṇavarman translation.)

Endnotes to the Guṇavarman Edition

1. As noted in the introduction to this volume, although the king in question here may indeed have been a "friend" of Nāgārjuna in the loose sense of the term, it is Nāgārjuna who adopts in this letter of instruction the role of the "good spiritual friend" (*kalyāṇa-mitra*) or "spiritual guide" and it is for that reason I render the Sanskrit title, *Suhṛllekha*, as "Letter *from* a Friend," and not as "Letter *to* a Friend" (as has been the case with most of the English translations originating with the Tibetan). Indeed, it is Nāgārjuna who is the *ārya*, not the King. Only an *ārya* can be relied upon to be one's friend in this and all future lives. The king, "friend" that he might be for the time being, might just as easily change into a deadly enemy with a change of circumstances (say, were he to convert to another religion, for instance) or a change of lifetimes. I suppose it should be noted that there is nothing in the Sanskrit title which defines it as intending either "from" or "to." Restricting it to one interpretation or the other is an artifact of having to produce a rendering into English.
2. "Muni" is an alternate designation for the Buddha.
3. The "recollections" vary in the number of components taught. For example, in *Mppu*, Nāgārjuna explains that sutra's list of "eight recollections" which, in addition to these six, includes "the breath," and "death." See my translation of *Nāgārjuna on the Eight Recollections*.
4. The "Three Jewels" are the Buddha, the Dharma, and the Ārya Sangha.
5. Nāgārjuna makes it clear elsewhere (In *Mppu*, in his discussion of the recollections) that this refers not just to "giving," but also to the "giving up" or "relinquishing" of the afflictions.
6. The ten good karmic deeds involve abstention from: killing, stealing, sexual misconduct (the three of the body), lying, harsh speech, divisive speech, lewd or frivolous speech (the four of the mouth), covetousness, hatefulness, and wrong views (the three of the mind). Nāgārjuna elsewhere (in his commentary on the ten bodhisattva grounds) holds forth on the path of the ten good karmic deeds at great length, pointing that they are the basis for the realization of all of the fruits of the Buddhist paths up to and including buddhahood.
7. "The three types of karma" is a reference to physical, verbal, and mental deeds. They are specified individually in all later editions (SV, YJ, and T).

8. "Fields of merit" is a metaphor for karmically potent recipients of giving. It refers to the fact that giving gifts to others, particularly to those of highly-evolved spiritual station, is, karmically speaking, like planting seeds of merit in an especially fertile field (the most fertile "field" being a buddha). These are bound to "sprout" and bear fruit in this and later lives as fortunate karmic outcomes involving easy acquisition of wealth, long life, and so forth. The metaphor is standard in all Buddhist traditions.

9. Lest the latter half of the verse seem obscure, the meaning is this: Of all of one's possessions, it is only one's giving which has the ability to travel along from life to life like a close companion.

10. Although the perfection of patience is in precisely correct order here, this edition alone makes a separate statement here about the qualities of patience and the Buddha's proclaiming its superiority. All three others merely list it with the other remaining perfections. YJ, SV, and T all have this very statement by the Buddha about the specific qualities of patience as occurring about a half dozen verses later.

11. All three later editions (SV, YJ, T) make direct or oblique reference to filial reverence for parents placing one in close relational proximity to the Brahma Heaven King.

12. All later editions indicate the next-life karmic reward to be celestial rebirth, with T being more euphemistic. Framed in terms of the ultimate goal of the Buddhist path, aspiration for celestial rebirth is basically considered to be wrong view in all schools of Buddhism. That said, N himself recommends it elsewhere (in *Mppu* and in *Bodhisaṃbhāra-śāstra*) as a "fallback" expedient teaching option for those who are incapable of relating to the idea of the renunciation so essential to high-level realization of any of the bodhi paths described by the Buddha. The saving grace of celestial rebirth for such karmic profiles is that it at least postpones plummeting once again into the three wretched destinies, thus increasing the chance that dedication to the Path may yet be adopted during the interim.

13. Obviously, sexual relations within the bounds of marriage is not proscribed for householders. The reference here is to short-term voluntary training for lay people through the skillful means of the eight precepts, usually taken only for single day or, alternately for six set days each month. See the very specific note which follows.

14. The Tibetan alone mentions refraining from wearing jewelry.

15. These eight precepts constitute the layperson's training regimen in the observance of enhanced moral virtue. They are commonly observed according to three different patterns, this after formally accepting them in a bhikshu-administered ceremony: for one day only, from

the first to the fifteenth day of the twelfth lunar month, or, in the more standard form known as the *upavāsa*, on the eighth, fourteenth, fifteenth, twenty-third, twenty-ninth, and thirtieth days of each lunar month. See my translation of *Nāgārjuna on the Perfection of Moral Virtue* for a more extended discussion of all of the specifics involved in the eight-precepts *upavāsa*.

16. It is this edition alone which makes specific reference to the eight precepts constituting a cause for the eventual realization of nirvāṇa.
17. The five objects of desire are explained either as the five objects of the five basic sense faculties or as wealth, sex, fame, food, and sleep.
18. Aṅgulimāla was searching for his one-thousandth murder victim when the Buddha brought him to his senses, whereupon he gained arhatship.
19. Sundarananda, formerly intractably attached to sensual enjoyments, renounced them after the Buddha showed him the long-term karmic effects, whereupon his cultivation led him to arhatship.
20. Śamā was a poverty-stricken woman who, through great industriousness in making offerings to the Sangha and in cultivating the eight precepts left behind her difficult circumstances and became a first-stage arhat (*srota-āpanna*) (T01.202.370a-c).
21. YJ and T differ on their identification of the exemplary cases. SV mentions no specific names.
22. It's common to interpret this common Buddhist analogy as pointing to leprosy, but leprosy is not marked by itching as a cardinal symptom. Also, it is caused by bacteria, not by parasitic mites. The Chinese characters used to translate the Sanskrit in all three editions indicate "scabies" which does indeed involve extreme itching created by the boring of the scabies mite and the ensuing allergic reaction.
23. In his *Ratnāvalī* (*Strand of Jewels*), Nāgārjuna makes this idea clearer still:
    Just as scratching an itch might be thought pleasurable,
    When having no itch is most pleasant of all,
    So too it is with pleasures linked to desire,
    For those free of desire are the happiest of all.
    (寶行王正論 / T25.1656.497a17-8)
24. Although the literal meaning of the Chinese characters (不淨) is in fact "impure," that is oftentimes a mere "stock" translation adopted by Sino-Buddhism for the Sanskrit *aśubha* which means "unlovely." In the absence of any proof of the actual Sanskrit antecedents here, it doesn't hurt to employ both concepts in the contemplation. Contemplation of the thirty-two (or thirty-six) parts of the body or of the nine stages of a corpse's deterioration makes both ideas abundantly clear.

25. Nāgārjuna is in no way suggesting that the King should dispense with other recommended practices for accumulating merit and wisdom. He is merely pointing to the superior potency of analytic contemplation in defeating delusions (such as the lust-based attachments just discussed) and in fathoming the ultimate reality of any given phenomenon.
26. These "eight worldly dharmas," otherwise known as "the eight winds" are: gain and loss, disgrace and esteem, praise and blame, and suffering and happiness.
27. "Muni" is an alternative honorific reference for the Buddha. The relevant meanings in Sanskrit, per the *Monier-Williams Sanskrit-English Dictionary*: "Saint, sage, seer, ascetic, monk, hermit."

    "The seven valuables of the Āryas" (*ārya-dhana*) is a commonly encountered list in both the *Āgamas* and the Mahāyāna Sutras.

    The *bodhimaṇḍala* is the site of enlightenment. In the case of the Buddha, it refers to the spot beneath the Bodhi Tree where he manifest realization of the utmost, right, and perfect enlightenment exclusive to buddhas.

    The "fruits" of the *bodhimaṇḍala* is a reference to the "fruits of the Path." In the case of the individual-liberation vehicle, this refers to any of the four stages of arhatship and also to pratyekabuddhahood. In the case of the universal-liberation vehicle, the reference is to the utmost, right, and perfect enlightenment of a buddha.
28. Emending the text by adopting the "six" of all other editions in favor of the "seven" found in this edition. The corruption could have easily have originated with mere scribal error. It's also possible that the "seven" resulted from a misreading of Guṇavarman's sometimes ornate Chinese style, with the result that some editor along the way mistakenly altered the text to fit seven categories erroneously thought be listed in this *śloka*.
29. All other editions insert at this point a discussion of the various types of bad and good wives which this GV edition places at the very end of this text, more or less as an addendum included right before the very last summarizing statement in the entire text.
30. I find no correlate of this verse in any of the other three editions. Here with the mention of "the abstinence rite," we have a reference to the eight-fold *upavāsa* training regimen for lay people. These eight precepts constitute the layperson's training regimen in the observance of enhanced moral virtue. They are commonly observed according to three different patterns, this after formally accepting them in a bhikshu-administered ceremony: for one day only, from the first to the fifteenth day of the twelfth lunar month, or, in the more standard form known as the *upavāsa*, on the eighth, fourteenth, fifteenth,

twenty-third, twenty-ninth, and thirtieth days of each lunar month. See my translation of *Nāgārjuna on the Perfection of Moral Virtue* for a more extended discussion of all of the specifics involved in the eight-precepts *upavāsa*.

31. GV's edition is alone in all of the editions in making a five-fold division of the periods of the night.
32. These four mind-training states are known as the "four immeasurable minds" (*apramāṇa-citta*) and are also referred to as the "four abodes of Brahmā" (*brahma-vihāra*). For an extensive discussion of this topic and the differences in their cultivation by individual-liberation and universal-liberation practitioners, see my translation of *Nāgārjuna on the Four Immeasurable Minds* under separate cover.
33. Of course rebirth in the heavens is considered to be problematic in Buddhism, this because it keeps one trapped in uncontrolled cyclic births and deaths. Hence, rather than allow undedicated merit to propel one to celestial rebirth, it is recommended that one single-mindedly resolve to strive for liberation from cyclic existence and dedicate all karmic merit to that higher goal. This disinclination to opt for celestial rebirth is shared by both individual-liberation and universal-liberation doctrines.
34. The five forms of erroneous conduct refer most likely to killing, stealing, sexual misconduct, lying, and consumption of intoxicants. The case for this is particularly strong because the five precepts and their opposites were only just mentioned directly above. That said, the Yijing and Tibetan editions both specifically reference the five hindrances. SV refers to "the thieves operating in the darkness of the five aggregates."
35. The five root-faculties are: faith, vigor, mindfulness, concentration, and wisdom. When fully developed, they are referred to as the "five powers."
36. The eight sufferings are: birth, aging, sickness, death, estrangement from the loved, proximity to what is hated, inability to gain what one seeks, the suffering inherent in the five aggregates.
37. The text recites here a short list of wrong views on the origins of the phenomena upon which "self" is imputed, then concludes with the most crucial three of the twelve causal links figuring in the perpetuation of a seeming karmic continuity. GV translates the name of the Īśvara god into Chinese which, if translated in turn into English, would produce the clumsy and distracting "the god Sovereignly Independent" or some such. Hence I simply reconstruct the Sanskrit. Although "aggregates" are not specified as the antecedent of "those dharmas" in the text, that they are intended is obvious from the

previous *śloka*.

The last three lines ("Absent any specific cause or condition, they are then destroyed. Great King, having realized the nature of such causes, One should light the lamp of wisdom and dispel the darkness of ignorance.") are not found in any of the other three editions of this text.

38. This analogy originates with the Buddha. There is but one blind turtle and it rises to the surface of the ocean but once every hundred years. There is only one yoke floating randomly around on the world's oceans. The turtle happens to poke its head up in just the right way that it is as if harnessed in it. This describes the difficulty of regaining human rebirth having once fallen down into the realm of animals.
39. A "central land" is for the most part defined as such by the availability of the Dharma and the "good spiritual friend." The "good spiritual friend" (*kalyāṇa-mitra*) is in most cases an artful term of reference for one's guru or "spiritual guide."
40. "Three realms" refers here to the many levels of rebirth taken on in the desire realm, form realm, and formless realm.
41. The implication here is that one's past-life mother may become this life's daughter, sister, or wife, a past-life enemy may become this life's brother or son, and so forth.
42. The continuous "circle" created by the wheel-shaped illusion emanating from a twirling firebrand is such that one cannot find any beginning point or ending point on it. This is a common analogy in Buddhism in general and in Nāgārjuna's writings in particular. It has deeper metaphysical meaning in relation to emptiness of inherent existence, the unreal basis for continuity of time, etc.
43. The five signs are explicitly stated in the YJ text:
    They become weary of their seats, their clothes become stained,
    The luster of their bodies deteriorates,
    Their armpits begin to perspire,
    And their aging floral chaplets start to wither. (T32.1674.753c08-9)
44. "Non-intermittent Hells" is a Chinese translation of the Avīci Hells.
45. Adopting the variant of 念 for 今 found in four other editions. An obvious scribal error.
46. The implication here is that just such faults are what lie behind being reborn among the *asuras*.
47. Perhaps one should be aware that the seven limbs of bodhi vary somewhat from text to text in the way they are listed. Basically, they are: dharmic analysis, vigor, joy, buoyant mental ease (*praśrabdhi*), mindfulness, concentration, and, depending on the scripture, either "wisdom," or the "equanimity" associated with the formative-factor

aggregate (as opposed to the equanimity with regard to the "feelings" aggregate which is so important in the acquisition of the dhyānas). The role of formative-factor equanimity in wisdom should be fairly obvious, however. Hence the difference between the two lists is relatively insignificant.

48. The fourteen are: Are the World and the self eternal, non-eternal, both, or neither?; Do the World and the self come to an end, or not, or both, or neither?; Does the Buddha continue to exist after his nirvāṇa, or not, or both, or neither?; Are the body and the soul identical or different? The Buddha deemed that answering these questions would serve no purpose, not least because they were like asking, "How much milk can one obtain from a bull's horn?" and hence would not conduce to awakening.

49. "Name-and-form" is a term referencing the mental ("name") and physical ("form") aggregates upon which personhood is typically imputed. "Feeling" is of six types corresponding to the six sense faculties. It is often misconstrued as referencing just physical sensation or just emotional "feelings." In fact it refers to both. Vasubandhu makes this quite clear in his *Abhidharma-kośa-bāṣyam*.

50. "Lion of the Āryas" is a reference to the Buddha himself.

51. The four truths: suffering, its origination, its cessation, the Path [to its cessation].

52. The eight-fold path of the Āryas: Right views, right thought, right speech, right action, right livelihood, right effort, right mindfulness, right meditative discipline.

53. The "three karmas" are the actions of body, mouth, and mind.

54. The SV translation specifies here "the four floods" (*catur-ogha*). These are: views (*dṛṣṭi-ogha*), desire (*kāma-ogha*), "becoming / existence" (*bhava-ogha*), and ignorance (*avidyā-ogha*).

Letter From a Friend (The *Suhṛllekha*)
Edition Two: The Saṅghavarman Translation

Dharma Essentials Verses for the Exhortation of Kings
By Nāgārjuna Bodhisattva

Translated by the Indian Tripiṭaka Master Saṅghavarman
During the Early Song Dynasty (circa 434 CE)

English Translation by Bhikshu Dharmamitra

简体字	正體字
劝发诸王要偈	勸發諸王要偈
龙树菩萨撰	龍樹菩薩撰
宋天竺三藏[1]僧伽跋摩译	宋天竺三藏[1]僧伽跋摩譯
明胜功德王	明勝功德王
我无馀求想	我無餘求想
诸佛所说法	諸佛所說法
庄严要何义	莊嚴要何義
略撰贤圣颂	略撰賢聖頌
大王所宜闻	大王所宜聞
如以众杂木	如以眾雜木
造立如来像	造立如來像
智者恭敬礼	智者恭敬禮
依佛故[2]尊视	依佛故[2]尊視
我今以非辩	我今以非辯
[3]光宣真[4]实藏	[3]光宣真[4]實藏
慧者应信乐	慧者應信樂
依法听所述	依法聽所述
大王虽数闻	大王雖數聞
如来梵音说	如來梵音說
胜悟由多闻	勝悟由多聞
屡闻则深信	屢聞則深信
如日照素质	如日照素質
岂不增其鲜	豈不增其鮮
三宝施戒天	三寶施戒天
最胜说六念	最勝說六念
随顺诸功德	隨順諸功德
如实善观察	如實善觀察

Letter from a Friend[1]

Dharma Essentials Verses for the Exhortation of Kings
By Nāgārjuna Bodhisattva
Translated by the Early Song Indian Tripiṭaka Master Saṇghavarman

I. Introduction and Encouragement to Pay Due Attention

1 (T1)

O King of illustrious and supreme merit,
I have no other aspiration
Than to set forth in the Dharma proclaimed by the Buddhas
What is the import of the essentials for adornment [of the Path].
This summarizing selection of verses from the Worthies and Āryas
Is deserving of the King's attention.

2 (T2)

Just as when one uses any of the various types of wood
To create an image of the Tathāgata,
The wise would respectfully bow there in reverence
And, because it is based on the Buddha's likeness, would venerate it,

3

So too, even though I now ineloquently
Elucidate [teachings from] the treasury of reality,
The intelligent should, with faith and happiness,
Acquiesce in what is written here in reliance on Dharma.

4 (T3)

Although the Great King may have repeatedly
Heard the discourse originating with the Tathāgata's brahman voice,[2]
Supreme understanding arises from extensive learning.
If one hears it repeatedly, then one develops deep faith.
This is comparable to when the moon shines on something white.[3]
How could it not enhance the freshness of its appearance?

II. The Main Doctrinal Section
  01. The Six Recollections

5 (T4)

The Three Jewels,[4] giving,[5] moral virtue, and the heavens—
The Victorious One (*jina*)[6] described them as the six recollections.[7]
They conduce to the creation of every sort of meritorious quality.
Make them the object of skillful reality-based contemplation.[8]

简体字	正體字
身口意常行 清净十业道 远酒不醉乱 离[5]邪修正命	身口意常行 清淨十業道 遠酒不醉亂 離[5]邪修正命
知财五家分 无常不牢固 惠施诸有德 贫苦及亲属 所生常随逐 布施为最胜	知財五家分 無常不牢固 惠施諸有德 貧苦及親屬 所生常隨逐 布施為最勝
不断亦不灭 不离不望果 如是诸净戒 宜应善受持 是则为良[6]田 生诸功德故	不斷亦不滅 不離不望果 如是諸淨戒 宜應善受持 是則為良[6]田 生諸功德故
施戒忍精进 禅定无量慧 是诸波罗蜜 慧者当修习 能度三有海 逮得牟尼尊	施戒忍精進 禪定無量慧 是諸波羅蜜 慧者當修習 能度三有海 逮得牟尼尊
若人孝父母 至心尽供养 是名礼教门 清净天胜族 名闻远流布 舍身生天上	若人孝父母 至心盡供養 是名禮教門 清淨天勝族 名聞遠流布 捨身生天上

02. The Ten Good Karmic Deeds, Abandoning Intoxicants, Right Livelihood

6 (T5)

In body, mouth, and mind, constantly practice
Purity in the path of the ten [good] karmic deeds.[9]
Abandon intoxicants. Do not be thrown into disorder by inebriation.
Abandon what is wrong as you cultivate right livelihood.

03. The Six Perfections (*pāramitā*)

7 (T6)

Realize that wealth, destined to be divided among five beneficiaries,[10]
Is impermanent and thus is not durable.
Give with kindness to those possessing virtues,
To the poor and suffering, and to relatives and retinue.
Of all one produces which might constantly follow on after us,
It is giving which is most supreme.

8 (T7)

As [karmic effects] cannot be either cut off or destroyed,
One can neither escape nor simply hope for particular karmic effects.
This being so, the moral precepts
Are such as one should see fit to skillfully accept and uphold.
If one acts accordingly, they become an especially fine "merit field,"[11]
This because they produce all of the meritorious qualities.

9 (T8)

As for giving, moral virtue, patience, vigor,
Dhyāna meditation, and the immeasurable wisdom,
All of these pāramitās
Are such as the wise should cultivate.
They can to take one across the sea of the three realms of existence,[12]
Ensuring success in becoming one honored among the *munis*.[13]

04. Filial Respect for Parents

10 (T9)

If a person treats his father and mother with filial respect
And, with utmost sincerity, exhaustively makes offerings to them
This serves as a gateway into reverence for the teachings
And brings about inclusion in the superior clan of the purity heavens.
One's reputation spreads far and wide
And, when one relinquishes this body, he is born in the heavens.

简体字	正體字
离杀盗婬欺 饮酒及三枝 成就八分齐 随顺诸佛学 舍身生六天 所欲悉随意	離殺盜婬欺 飲酒及三枝 成就八分(齊)[齋] 隨順諸佛學 捨身生六天 所欲悉隨意
悭谄幻伪慢 懈怠贪恚痴 族姓好容色 少壮多闻乐 如是诸迷惑 当视如怨家	慳諂幻偽慢 懈怠貪恚癡 族姓好容色 少壯多聞樂 如是諸迷惑 當視如怨家
若修不放逸 是则不死路 放逸为死径 世尊之所说 为增善法故 当修不放逸	若修不放逸 是則不死路 放逸為死徑 世尊之所說 為增善法故 當修不放逸
若人先为恶 后能不放逸 是则照世间 云除月光显	若人先為惡 後能不放逸 是則照世間 雲除月光顯
忍辱无与等 不随瞋恚心 佛说能远离 是得不还道	忍辱無與等 不隨瞋恚心 佛說能遠離 是得不還道

05. The Layperson's Eight-Precept *Upavāsa* Abstinence Rite

11 (T10-1)
Abandoning killing, stealing, sexual relations,[14]
Deception, intoxicants, and the other three transgressing factors—[15]
If one perfectly observes this eight-fold abstinence rite,[16]
One thereby accords with the training laid down by all buddhas.
On leaving this body, one is reborn in the six [desire realm] heavens
Where whatever one desires all manifests according to one's wishes.

06. Abandonment of Faults

12 (T12)
Miserliness, flattery, deceptiveness, falseness, pride,
Indolence, covetousness, hatefulness, delusion—
[Arrogance based on] caste, clan, on fine countenance or appearance,
On youthfulness, strength, extensive learning, or one's pleasures—
All such delusions as these
Should be seen as one's adversaries.

07. Non-Neglectfulness versus Neglectfulness

13 (T13)
If one cultivates non-neglectfulness,
This then constitutes the road to the deathless.
Neglectfulness is the path leading toward death.
This is as taught by the Bhagavān.
For the sake of increasing good dharmas,
One should cultivate non-neglectfulness.

14 (T14)
If a person who previously acted badly
Then afterwards becomes able to refrain from neglectfulness,
Then this brings a shining radiance into the world
As when clouds disperse and moonlight shines forth.

08. On the Special Importance of Patience and Relinquishing Hatefulness

15 (T15)
Patience has no peer.
In preventing one from following the hateful mind.
The Buddha declared that, if one is able to abandon [hatred],
This conduces to realization of the path of the non-returner.[17]

简体字	正體字
有瞋如画水 或如画土石 若说[7]超烦恼 初人则为胜 改恶修慈忍 第三则为上	有瞋如畫水 或如畫土石 若說[7]超煩惱 初人則為勝 改惡修慈忍 第三則為上
最胜说众生 三种善恶语 初名引人心 美言如饴蜜 次名真实语 犹如妙华敷	最勝說眾生 三種善惡語 初名引人心 美言如飴蜜 次名真實語 猶如妙華敷
后名不诚实 鄙浮如粪秽 慧者应分别 舍后修初二	後名不誠實 鄙浮如糞穢 慧者應分別 捨後修初二
从明明至终 从暗暗究竟 有从暗入明 或从明入冥 慧者应谛了 舍三升初明	從明明至終 從闇闇究竟 有從闇入明 或從明入冥 慧者應諦了 捨三昇初明
有人生似熟 或复熟似生 或二俱生熟 明者谛分别	有人生似熟 或復熟似生 或二俱生熟 明者諦分別

16 (T17)
When influenced by hatred, one may act as if drawing on water,
As if etching in the dirt, or as if carving on stone.
To speak of the best course of action for transcending afflictions,
The first person's actions would be supreme.
When turning from evil to cultivation of compassion and patience,
Following the third course of action is superior.

09. Three Kinds of Speech
17 (T18)
The Victorious One (*jina*) declared that beings
Use three different kinds of good or bad discourse.
The first is that which leads forth a person's mind.
Such pleasing words are comparable to rice-honey.[18]
The next is truthful discourse.
This is comparable to the blooming of marvelous flowers.

18
The last is that which is not truthful.
This is base, groundless, and comparable to feces.
The wise should make these distinctions,
Abandoning the latter while cultivating the first two.

10. Criteria for Evaluating Both Self and Prospective Associates
A. Four Types of Personal Destinies Linked to Brilliance or Darkness
19 (T19)
One may go from present brilliance to being brilliant in the end,
Or go from present darkness to abiding in darkness at the very end.
There are those who go from present darkness into later brilliance
And those who go from present brilliance into later darkness.
The wise should truly understand this,
Dispense with three of them, ascending to the first type of brilliance.

B. Four Types of Persons Compared to a Mango's Ripeness
20 (T20)
There are those [mangoes] which, though unripe, appear ripe,
Those which, though ripe, appear unripe, and
Those which, both in fact and appearance, are either unripe or ripe.
One possessed of brilliance should carefully make these distinctions.

简体字	正體字
不视他妻色 视则母女想 如是犹生惑 当修不净观	不視他妻色 視則母女想 如是猶生惑 當修不淨觀
心意善驰乱 当勤善守持 如人护胜闻 宝藏爱子命	心意善馳亂 當勤善守持 如人護勝聞 寶藏愛子命
当观五欲乐 犹如恶毒蛇 怨憎及[8]刀火 方便修厌离	當觀五欲樂 猶如惡毒蛇 怨憎及[8]刀火 方便修厭離
五欲生非义 犹如频婆果 覆相善欺诳 缚人住生死 智者当观察 弃舍勿染污	五欲生非義 猶如頻婆果 覆相善欺誑 縛人住生死 智者當觀察 棄捨勿染污
诸根常轻躁 驰散六尘境 若能善调伏 是则大勇健	諸根常輕躁 馳散六塵境 若能善調伏 是則大勇健
是身为行厕 九道常流秽 穿漏难可满 薄皮隐不净 愚者为所欺 智[9]士当厌离	是身為行廁 九道常流穢 穿漏難可滿 薄皮隱不淨 愚者為所欺 智[9]士當厭離

11. On Dealing with Desire
A. On Guarding the Mind

21 (T21)

Do not look upon the physical form of others' wives.
If one lays eyes on one, reflect upon her as one's mother or daughter.
If, even doing this, one still generates delusions,
One should cultivate the contemplation of impurity.

22 (T22)

The mind easily runs off and becomes confused.
One should be diligent and skillful in guarding and restraining it,
Doing so just as one guards a superior reputation,
A treasury of jewels, a cherished son, or one's life.

23

One should contemplate the five types of desire
As comparable to a fearsome and venomous snake,
To detested adversaries, or to swords and fire,
Thus using skillful means to cultivate renunciation.

B. On the Hazards Inherent in Desire

24 (T23)

The five desires create circumstances contrary to principle.
They are analogous to the *bimba* fruit.[19]
They hide the true character of things, easily deceive one,
And imprison a person in the domain of birth and death.
The wise person should analytically contemplate them
And renounce them. He must not become defiled by them.

C. On the Superior Valor in Controlling Desire

25 (T24)

The sense faculties tend to be constantly restive and agitated,
Running off and scattering in the realms of the six sense objects.
If one is able to skillfully train and discipline them,
One becomes thereby a great and valiant stalwart.

D. On the Unloveliness of the Body

26 (T25)

This body is a moving outhouse,
Constantly streaming filth from nine apertures.
As they flow on out, it is difficult to keep it full.
A thin skin disguises its impurity.[20]
The foolish are deceived by it.
The wise gentleman should turn away from it in disgust.

简体字	正體字
如人病疥虫 向火欲除患 少乐后苦增 贪欲亦如是 能善知欲过 从是离众苦 欲见第一义 佛说观缘起 应当勤修习 最胜无过是 族姓身端严 多闻自[10]缨络 若不修戒慧 此则非殊胜 能具二功德 无三犹奇特 利衰及毁誉 称讥与苦乐 八法不倾动 是则为圣王 莫为诸天神 沙门婆罗门 宗亲及宾客 害生造恶业 命终入地狱 独受彼不代 若人作恶业 不即受楚毒 命终受苦报 后悔将何及	如人病疥蟲 向火欲除患 少樂後苦增 貪欲亦如是 能善知欲過 從是離眾苦 欲見第一義 佛說觀緣起 應當勤修習 最勝無過是 族姓身端嚴 多聞自[10]纓絡 若不修戒慧 此則非殊勝 能具二功德 無三猶奇特 利衰及毀譽 稱譏與苦樂 八法不傾動 是則為聖王 莫為諸天神 沙門婆羅門 宗親及賓客 害生造惡業 命終入地獄 獨受彼不代 若人作惡業 不即受楚毒 命終受苦報 後悔將何及

27 (T26)
Just as when someone afflicted with itch-inducing parasites[21]
Draws close to a fire, wishing to be rid of his distress,
But after a brief sense of pleasure, the pain only increases—
So too it is when indulging the desires.[22]

12. In Praise of Contemplation-Based Insight, Wisdom, and Moral Virtue
28 (T27)
If one is able to well understand the faults inhering in the desires,
Then from this he may succeed in abandoning the many sufferings.
If one wishes to realize the ultimate truth,
The Buddha declared one should contemplate conditioned arising.
One should diligently cultivate this practice
For it is the most supreme practice. There are none which surpass it.[23]

29 (T28)
Though well-born, possessed of fine and attractive physical form,
Abundant learning, and graced as if by a jeweled necklace,
Still, if one fails to cultivate moral virtue and wisdom,
This does not qualify one as being especially superior.
If, however, one is able to embody these latter two qualities
Even absent the former three, one is still especially distinguished.

13. On Avoiding the Eight Worldly Dharmas and Offenses Inspired by Others
30 (T29)
Gain and loss, esteem and disgrace,
Praise and blame, happiness and suffering—
If one is not even slightly shaken by these eight dharmas,
This in itself makes one a king among the Āryas.

31 (T30)
Do not, influenced by some god, spirit,
Śramaṇa, brahman,
Clansman, or visitor,
Allow yourself to harm any being or engage in any evil karmic deed.
When one's life comes to an end and one plummets into the hells,
One endures that retribution alone, for they will not stand in for you.

14. On the Delayed Arrival of Karmic Retributions
32 (T31)
If a person commits evil karmic deeds,
He does not straightaway suffer the fierce punishments they entail.
Only at the end of this life does one then reap the bitter retribution.
Though one may finally regret it, of what use will that be then?

信戒施多闻 智慧有惭愧 佛说不共财 馀财一切共	信戒施多聞 智慧有慚愧 佛說不共財 餘財一切共
博弈大聚会 懒惰习恶友 饮酒纵昏荡 夜游无羞耻 此六污名称 智者应远离	博弈大聚會 懶惰習惡友 飲酒縱昏蕩 夜遊無羞恥 此六污名稱 智者應遠離
知足为大财 世尊所称说 若能修知足 虽贫[1]贱大富 譬如多头龙 多头则多苦	知足為大財 世尊所稱說 若能修知足 雖貧[1]賤大富 譬如多頭龍 多頭則多苦
自性结恨深 是名怨家妇 傲慢不承顺 名为轻夫妇	自性結恨深 是名怨家婦 傲慢不承順 名為輕夫婦
费用夫主财 是则名贼妇 慎哉贤丈夫 宜远此三妇	費用夫主財 是則名賊婦 慎哉賢丈夫 宜遠此三婦
随顺为姊妹 爱乐为善友 安慰则为母 随意为婢使 此四贤良妻 则是[2](夫)[天]眷属	隨順為姊妹 愛樂為善友 安慰則為母 隨意為婢使 此四賢良妻 則是[2](夫)[天]眷屬
简体字	正體字

15. On the Āryas' Seven Forms of Wealth

33 (T32)

Faith, moral virtue, giving, abundant learning,
Wisdom, a sense of shame, and a sense of blame—
Buddha described these as the especially exclusive forms of wealth,
Whereas all other forms of wealth are held in common by everyone.[24]

16. On Six Coarse Faults to Be Eliminated

34 (T33)

Gambling, attending mass-entertainment gatherings,
Indolence, habitually consorting with bad friends,
Drinking intoxicants, indulging muddle-headed, licentious behavior,
Roaming about at night bereft of any sense of shame—
These six sully one's reputation.
The wise should abandon them.

17. In Praise of Being Easily Satisfied

35 (T34-5)

Being easily satisfied is a form of great wealth.
This is as declared by the Bhagavān.
If one is able to cultivate being easily satisfied,
Though poor and of low social status, one still possesses great riches.
[One who fails in this] is comparable to the many-headed dragon
Which, having many heads, experiences all the more suffering.

18. On the Various Sorts of Candidates for Marriage

36 (T36)

One who by nature cherishes deep resentment—
This type is known as the adversarial wife.
One who is arrogant and unaccommodating—
This type is known as the husband-slighting wife.

37

One who wastes the wealth generated by the husband—
This type is known as the plundering wife.
Take care! The worthy husband
Finds it fitting to avoid these three types of prospects for marriage.

38 (T37)

One so accommodating as to be like a sister,
One so cherishing and pleasing as to be like a fine friend,
One so comforting as to be like a mother,
Or one so compliant as to be like a maidservant—
Any of these four refined and good marriage prospects
Could be regarded as fitting for the retinue of a god.[25]

简体字	正體字
饮食为汤药 无贪恚痴服 唯为止身苦 勿为肥放逸	飲食為湯藥 無貪恚癡服 唯為止身苦 勿為肥放逸
昼则勤修业 初后夜亦然 中夜亦正念 无令空梦过	晝則勤修業 初後夜亦然 中夜亦正念 無令空夢過
慈悲喜舍心 日夜常修习 设未出世间 其福胜梵天	慈悲喜捨心 日夜常修習 設未出世間 其福勝梵天
离欲觉欢喜 苦乐修四禅 梵光净果实 受此诸天乐	離欲覺歡喜 苦樂修四禪 梵光淨果實 受此諸天樂
若人少行恶 广修无量善 如以一把盐 投之大恒水	若人少行惡 廣修無量善 如以一把鹽 投之大恒水
若人多行恶 少修净功德 如以多恶毒 置之小器食	若人多行惡 少修淨功德 如以多惡毒 置之小器食
五阴暗冥贼 劫人善珍宝 信五根力士 是能善守护	五陰闇冥賊 劫人善珍寶 信五根力士 是能善守護

Chapter 2: *The Saṅghavarman Suhṛllekha Translation*

19. On Moderation and Sensibility in Eating

39 (T38)

Food and drink serve as medicines
Which one ingests without indulging craving, aversion, or delusion.
They are taken solely to halt the sufferings of the body.
One must not partake of them in a way which increases negligence.

20. Exhortation to Encourage Diligence and Mindfulness

40 (T39)

One should cultivate diligently during the day
And should do so as well in the beginning and end of the night.
Even in the middle of the night, one must retain right mindfulness,
Not allowing it to uselessly pass by in dreams.

21. The Four Immeasurable Minds and Cultivation of the Dhyāna Absorptions

41 (T40)

Minds of kindness, compassion, sympathetic joy, and equanimity,
Are to be cultivated constantly throughout the day and night.
Even if one has not yet succeeded in transcending the world,
One's merit will become superior even to that of the God Brahmā.[26]

42 (T41)

If one abandons desire, awakens to joy and bliss,
And, in both suffering and happiness, cultivates the four dhyānas,
One enjoys bliss in the Brahma, Light-and-Sound, Universal Purity,
And Extensive Fruition Heavens as a consequence of that.[27]

22. On the Mitigating Effect of Predominant Goodness

43 (T43)

If someone commits but a few bad karmic deeds
While extensively cultivating countless good deeds,
This is analogous to taking a mere handful of salt
And tossing it into the waters of the Ganges.

44

If one commits numerous evil deeds
And cultivates but little in the way of pure meritorious qualities,
This is comparable to taking a large amount of deadly poison
And placing it into a small dish of food.[28]

23. The Five Aggregates as Thieves; The Five Roots and Powers as Guards

45 (T44-5)

The thieves operating in the darkness of the five aggregates
Steal away the precious jewels of a person's goodness.[29]
The soldiers of faith and the other five root-faculties and powers[30]
Which are well able to guard and protect them.

简体字	正體字
生老病死苦 所爱者别离 沦没不超度 斯由自业过	生老病死苦 所愛者別離 淪沒不超度 斯由自業過
求生天解脱 当[3]勤修正见 邪见虽行善 一切得苦果	求生天解脱 當[3]勤修正見 邪見雖行善 一切得苦果
无常苦不净 应当善观察 若不正思惟 四倒盲慧眼	無常苦不淨 應當善觀察 若不正思惟 四倒盲慧眼
端正色非我 我色亦非主 四阴亦复然 唯是空苦聚	端正色非我 我色亦非主 四陰亦復然 唯是空苦聚
非时非无因 亦非自性有 非自在天生 无明爱业起	非時非無因 亦非自性有 非自在天生 無明愛業起
身见戒取疑 是三障解脱 圣慧开脱门 自力不由他	身見戒取疑 是三障解脱 聖慧開脱門 自力不由他

24. Suffering, Its Origin, and Necessity of Right Views to Liberation
A. The Eight Sufferings and the Basis for Their Arising

46 (T46)

As for the sufferings of birth, aging, sickness, death,
Separation from what one loves, [and so forth],[31]
One's immersion in them and failing to cross beyond them
Is a consequence of one's own karmic transgressions.

B. The Necessity of Right Views to Liberation

47 (T47)

In seeking rebirth in the heavens or in seeking liberation,
One must diligently cultivate right views.
Even if one cultivates good deeds when possessed of wrong views,
Everything one does ends up producing results involving suffering.

C. The Four Right Views versus the Four Inverted Views

48 (T48)

Impermanence, suffering, impurity, [and non-self]—
One should skillfully employ them in analytic contemplation.
If one fails to maintain right thought,
The four inverted views will blind one's wisdom eye.

D. Right and Wrong Views on the Aggregates
1. The Absence of Any "Self" Associated with the Five Aggregates

49 (T49)

One's typical physical form is not a "self," [nor is self form],
Nor do either form or self serve as a host for existence of the other.[32]
So, too, with the other four aggregates.
[The merely-imputed "self"] is a mere aggregation empty of inherent
  existence and characterized by suffering.

2. On the Origins of the Aggregates

50 (T50)

[Aggregates] are not produced by time, not produced without a cause,
Not caused to exist as a function of their intrinsic nature,
And are not created by the Iśvara god.
They arise as a result of ignorance, craving, and karmic actions.[33]

E. Three Fetters Impeding Liberation; Necessity of Wisdom and Self-Reliance

51 (T51-2)

The view taking body as self, seizing on [non-beneficial] prohibitions,
And doubtfulness are three factors obstructing liberation.
The wisdom of the Āryas opens the gateway to liberation.
This is consummated by one's own efforts, not on account of others.

简体字	正體字
净戒学禅定 精勤修四(禅)[谛] 增上戒心慧 常当勤修学 诸戒智三昧 悉入三学中	淨戒學禪定 精勤修四(禪)[諦] 增上戒心慧 常當勤修學 諸戒智三昧 悉入三學中
身念处大力 佛说一乘道 常当系心念 方便善守护 若忘是正念 则失诸善法	身念處大力 佛說一乘道 常當繫心念 方便善守護 若忘是正念 則失諸善法
身命极浮脆 喻风吹水泡 梦觉难可保 出息无必[4]旋	身命極浮脆 喻風吹水泡 夢覺難可保 出息無必[4]旋
倏忽成微尘 当知无坚固 大地须弥海 七日皆烧然 廓然无遗烬 况复危脆身	倏忽成微塵 當知無堅固 大地須彌海 七日皆燒然 廓然無遺燼 況復危脆身
无常不可依 亦非覆护法 是身不可[5]怙 如何不生厌	無常不可依 亦非覆護法 是身不可[5]怙 如何不生厭
譬如海盲龟 值遇浮木孔 畜生复人身 难得复过是 如何人道中 不修胜果业	譬如海盲龜 值遇浮木孔 畜生復人身 難得復過是 如何人道中 不修勝果業

25. THE THREE TRAININGS

52 (T52-3)

Through purity in prohibitions, learning, and dhyāna concentration,
Exert intense diligence in cultivation of the four truths.[34]
The superior practice of moral virtue, concentration, and wisdom
Should be cultivated and studied with constancy and diligence.
All of the moral prohibitions, wisdom, and samādhis
Are entirely subsumed within these three trainings.

26. THE STATION OF MINDFULNESS WITH RESPECT TO THE BODY

53 (T54)

The great power of the station of mindfulness regarding the body
Was declared by Buddha to be [essential to the] single-vehicle path.
One should constantly anchor the mind's attention therein,
Employing expedient means to skillfully guard it.
If one forgets this right mindfulness,
Then one is bound to lose all good dharmas.

54 (T55)

One's physical life abides at the extreme of floating fragility.
In this, it is analogous to a water bubble blown by the wind.
On slipping into dreams, there is no guarantee one will ever awaken.
When exhaling, there is no certainty one's breath will ever return.

55 (T56-7)

It proceeds swiftly to mere dust.
One should realize it has no durability.
Even the great earth, Mount Sumeru, and the oceans
Will all be incinerated when the seven suns appear.
Then, throughout that vast expanse, nary a cinder will remain,
How much the less any trace of this vulnerable and fragile body?

56 (T58)

It is impermanent, undependable,
And affords neither shelter or protection.
This body cannot be relied upon.
How could one fail then to generate renunciation toward it?

57 (T59)

Just as with the case of some blind turtle out in the ocean chancing
To poke its head up through the opening in a floating wooden yoke,[35]
Return to human incarnation from the animal realm
Is even more rarely encountered than this.
How can one abiding in the path of human rebirth
Fail to cultivate the karma leading to the supreme fruits [of the Path]?

简体字	正體字
宝器盛粪秽 是则愚痴人 已得人身宝 而用造恶行 当知此士夫 极愚复过是	寶器盛糞穢 是則愚癡人 已得人身寶 而用造惡行 當知此士夫 極愚復過是
得生有道国 遭遇善知识 正见心成就 宿命有功德 四宝轮具足 能出生死路	得生有道國 遭遇善知識 正見心成就 宿命有功德 四寶輪具足 能出生死路
亲近善知识 具足修梵行 佛说如是人 心常得寂灭	親近善知識 具足修梵行 佛說如是人 心常得寂滅
邪见三恶趣 不闻佛法音 边地暗冥处 聋痖长寿天	邪見三惡趣 不聞佛法音 邊地闇冥處 聾瘂長壽天
王已离八难 得此无碍身 宜应修善业 方便求泥洹	王已離八難 得此無礙身 宜應修善業 方便求泥洹
生死长夜中 无量种种苦 展转作六亲 尊卑无常序	生死長夜中 無量種種苦 展轉作六親 尊卑無常序

58 (T60)

To fill up a jeweled vessel with the filth of feces
Is an action carried out by a fool.
Having already found the jewel of rebirth in a human body,
Were someone to then use it to commit evil actions—
One should realize such a person
Thereby reaches an even greater extreme of stupidity than this.

27. On the Circumstances Requisite for Cultivating the Path

59 (T61)

Having been born in a country possessing the Path,
Having encountered the good spiritual friend,[36]
Having developed a mind governed by right views,
And possessing merit generated in previous lives,
One is thus perfectly equipped with the four precious wheels[37]
And is thereby enabled to escape from the path of birth-and-death.

60 (T62)

As for those who have drawn close to the good spiritual friend
And perfectly cultivated the brahman conduct,[38]
The Buddha declared of such persons
That their minds will always realize quiescent cessation.[39]

28. Description of the Faults of Cyclic Existence
A. An Introductory General Description of Faults

61 (T63)

One guided by wrong views falls into the three wretched destinies,
Remains unable to hear the sound of the Buddha's Dharma,
Abides in the hinterlands' regions of darkness,
Becomes deaf, becomes mute, or inhabits the long-life heavens.[40]

62 (T64)

The King has already abandoned the eight difficulties[41]
And has gained this body abiding in unrestricted circumstances.
It is only fitting that he cultivate good karmic deeds,
And employ the expedient means through which one seeks nirvāṇa.

63 (T65-6)

Throughout the long night of cyclic births and deaths,
One undergoes countless sufferings of many different sorts.
As one courses on in it, manifesting as the six types of relatives,
There is no fixed basis ensuring honorable or inferior social station.

简体字	正體字
永劫生死中 未曾不为子 计饮慈母乳 量喻四大海 凡夫方受生 所饮复过是	永劫生死中 未曾不為子 計飲慈母乳 量喻四大海 凡夫方受生 所飲復過是
一人从本来 积骨高须弥 所经诸人天 大地微尘数	一人從本來 積骨高須彌 所經諸人天 大地微塵數
先作转轮王 后复为仆使 或上为帝释 诸天所奉事 下生粪土中 往反亦无[6]数	先作轉輪王 後復為僕使 或上為帝釋 諸天所奉事 下生糞土中 往反亦無[6]數
或时生天上 婇女极娱乐 目眩众妙色 耳闻万种声	或時生天上 婇女極娛樂 目眩眾妙色 耳聞萬種聲
触身皆细软 快乐难可名 后堕地狱中 苦毒靡不经 若生剑林树 身首随刃零	觸身皆細軟 快樂難可名 後墮地獄中 苦毒靡不經 若生劍林樹 身首隨刃零
或游须弥顶 升降随所念 与众天女俱 沐浴曼陀池	或遊須彌頂 昇降隨所念 與眾天女俱 沐浴曼陀池

64 (T67)
During an eternity of kalpas coursing in cyclic births and deaths,
One has never not taken on birth as an infant.
If one reckoned the amount of milk drunk from one's kindly mothers,
Its volume would compare to the waters of the four great oceans.
As a common person who will thenceforth take on yet more births,
The amount yet to be drunk shall be even greater than this.

65 (T68)
Any single person, from the beginning on forth to the present,
Has left an accumulation of bones rivaling Mount Sumeru's height.
The number of births passed through among humans and gods
Exceed the number of dust motes in the entire earth.

    B. ON IMPERMANENCE AND REVERSIBILITY OF OSTENSIBLY DESIRABLE EXISTENCES
66 (T69)
Having formerly been a wheel-turning king,
One later returns to become a slave.
Though one may ascend to become Śakra Devānām Indra
And be served by all of the other gods,
Still, one may then fall down to be reborn in a dunghill,
Going forth and coming back like this countless times.

67 (T70)
One may at times gain rebirth in the heavens
And enjoy ecstatic pleasures with consorts there.
One's eyes may be dazzled by all manner of marvelous forms
And one's ears may hear a myriad sorts of sounds.

68 (T71-2)
The contact experienced by the body is all smooth and soft
And the pleasures are so blissful, they are difficult even to describe.
Afterwards, however, one plummets down into the hells
Where there is no excruciating cruelty one avoids experiencing.
When one is reborn into the Sword-Forest [Hells],
One's head falls away as it encounters the blades.

69 (T73)
One may roam to the very summit of Mount Sumeru,
Experiencing the rising and falling adapting to one's thoughts.⁴²
Together with numerous heavenly maidens,
One bathes in the *mandārava* flower ponds.

简体字	正體字
宝华列庄严 清凉极快乐 复入沸灰河 烹煮悉糜烂 六[1]天五欲[2]欢 梵世离欲乐 [3]死入无择狱 备受众苦毒 或作日月天 光明照四域 后生黑暗狱 不自见其形 王当然慧灯 勿复随长冥 [4]八大地狱中 烧炙屠裂苦 备经众楚毒 无量不可譬 若人随痴惑 具造众恶业 出息未反间 闻是诸大苦 其心不惊怖 是则木石人 眼见报应[5]像 复闻智者说 彼[6]采佛经典 内心正思惟 则应大怖畏 何况身自经	寶華列莊嚴 清涼極快樂 復入沸灰河 烹煮悉糜爛 六[1]天五欲[2]歡 梵世離欲樂 [3]死入無擇獄 備受眾苦毒 或作日月天 光明照四域 後生黑闇獄 不自見其形 王當然慧燈 勿復隨長冥 [4]八大地獄中 燒炙屠裂苦 備經眾楚毒 無量不可譬 若人隨癡惑 具造眾惡業 出息未反間 聞是諸大苦 其心不驚怖 是則木石人 眼見報應[5]像 復聞智者說 彼[6]採佛經典 內心正思惟 則應大怖畏 何況身自經

70
Precious blossoms are arrayed there in adornment
As one experiences extremely blissful coolness.
One then enters once again the river of boiling ashes,
Where one is boiled and steamed till one's flesh falls away.

71 (T74)
One may enjoy the five desires in the six desire heavens
As well as desire-transcending bliss in the Brahma-World Heaven.
Still, when one dies, one may enter the Non-Intermittent Hells[43]
There to suffer in full measure many sorts of agonizing cruelties.

72 (T75)
One may become a deity of the sun or moon
Whose radiance illuminates the four continents.
Still, one may afterwards enter the darkness of the hells
Where [it is so dark] one cannot even see his own body.

C. The Hells

73 (T76)
The King should light the lamp of wisdom.
Do not continue to follow the path of everlasting darkness.
In the eight great hells,
One is dealt the pain of being roasted, slaughtered, and split open.

74 (T77-82)
One passes in full measure through many excruciating punishments
Which are countless and impossible to describe even by analogy.
If a person courses along in stupidity and delusion,
He creates in repletion a multitude of evil karmic deeds.

75 (T83)
If someone merely hears of all of these immense sufferings
And then, in the moment it takes to exhale a breath,
Has not yet been struck with a terrified mind,
He must certainly be a man made of wood or stone.

76 (T84)
If someone sees with his own eyes images of the retributions,
Hears a knowledgeable person describe them,
Or else reads a choice Buddhist scripture
And then correctly contemplates this matter in his own mind,
He should then be struck with great terror.
How much the more would this be so were one to undergo it himself.

简体字	正體字
一切受苦中 无择最大苦 一切受乐中 爱尽第一乐 日夜各三时 三百枪贯身 欲比无择苦 百千倍非譬 无量诸楚毒 求死不可得 受罪百千岁 恶业尽乃毕 不净苦果报 身口业为种 不种则不有 王[7]宜断苦本 若堕畜生趣 系缚杀害苦 贪害狂乱心 怨结更相食 或为取珠宝 毛尾皮肉骨 由是丧身命 解剥断截痛 骏足有大力 穿[8]颈服乘苦 狂逸不[9]调驯 策勒而榜楚	一切受苦中 無擇最大苦 一切受樂中 愛盡第一樂 日夜各三時 三百槍貫身 欲比無擇苦 百千倍非譬 無量諸楚毒 求死不可得 受罪百千歲 惡業盡乃畢 不淨苦果報 身口業為種 不種則不有 王[7]宜斷苦本 若墮畜生趣 繫縛殺害苦 貪害狂亂心 怨結更相食 或為取珠寶 毛尾皮肉骨 由是喪身命 解剝斷截痛 駿足有大力 穿[8]頸服乘苦 狂逸不[9]調馴 策勒而榜楚

77 (T85)
Of all of the forms of suffering,
The Non-Intermittent Hells have the most extremely great suffering.
Of all of the forms of bliss,
The ending of desire is the foremost type of bliss.

78 (T86)
If one were to endure three times each day and night
Being impaled by three hundred spears,
And wished to compare it to the Non-Intermittent Hell's sufferings,
It could not compare even if multiplied a hundred thousand times.

79 (T87)
One undergoes countless forms of excruciating torture
And, though one might wish to die, that cannot come to pass.
One undergoes punishments for a hundred thousand years
And only once one's evil karma is exhausted does it finally end.

80 (T88)
The painful retribution arising from impurity
Finds its seeds in the karmic actions of one's body and mouth.
If one does not plant them, then they do not come into existence.
It is only fitting that the King cut off the roots of suffering.

D. THE ANIMALS
81 (T89)
If one falls down into the path of animal rebirth,
One endures the suffering of being tied up, killed, or injured.
As desire and injuriousness craze and disorder the mind,
Enemies are made who then consume each other there.

82 (T90)
It may happen that, due to quests for pearls,
Furs, tails, hides, flesh, or bones,
One becomes bound on these accounts to lose one's life,
Enduring then the pain of being cut open, skinned, or hacked apart.

83
Being swift-footed or possessed of great strength,
One may suffer from being yoked, bearing loads, or being ridden.
If one is wild, disobedient, or untrained,
One may be subjected to the whip, to reins, and to flogging.

简体字	正體字
饿鬼思饮食 所念未曾有 饥渴寒热[10]迫 长夜无休息	餓鬼思飲食 所念未曾有 飢渴寒熱[10]迫 長夜無休息
或身如[11]大山 咽口若针锋 饥渴内烧燃 对食食无从	或身如[11]大山 咽口若針鋒 飢渴內燒燃 對食食無從
或见粪脓唾 群走竞驰趣 到则自然灭 望绝增苦恼	或見糞膿唾 群走競馳趣 到則自然滅 望絕增苦惱
饥渴煎其[12]内 瘤瘿发痈疽 更共相撮搏 龃[13]龇唼脓血	飢渴煎其[12]內 瘤癭發癰疽 更共相撮搏 齟[13]齜唼膿血
羸[14]疮皮骨连 裸形被长发 身长若枯木 [15]炽焰从口出 还自焚其身 状烧多罗树	羸[14]瘡皮骨連 裸形被長髮 身長若枯木 [15]熾焰從口出 還自焚其身 狀燒多羅樹
处夏希夜凉 月光增其热 在冬思昼温 日出[16]逾冰结 向树果即消 趣河水辄竭	處夏希夜涼 月光增其熱 在冬思晝溫 日出[16]逾冰結 向樹果即消 趣河水輒竭
经万五千岁 业持命不绝 久受无量苦 斯由宿罪缘	經萬五千歲 業持命不絕 久受無量苦 斯由宿罪緣

E. The Hungry Ghosts

84 (T91)
Though the hungry ghosts obsess on obtaining food and drink,
They never succeed in obtaining anything they wish for.
They are driven along by hunger, thirst, cold, and heat,
Continuing ceaselessly on like that into the long night [of the future].

85 (T92)
Their bodies may become as huge as a great mountain
While their throats remain as narrow as a needle.
Their hunger and thirst always burn within them
And, though they may encounter food, they have no way to obtain it.

86
They may lay eyes on excrement, pus, or spittle
And run together toward it, struggling as they race,
Only to see it spontaneously disappear just as they reach it.
The dashing of hopes only serves to increase their bitter afflictions.

87 (T94)
Hunger and thirst so boil within them that,
When one of their goiters develops external ulcers,
The others swarm around, pounce on him,
And sink their teeth into it to suck the pus and blood.

88 (T93)
They are emaciated, covered with sores, but skin and bones,
And naked, robed only in their long hair.
Their bodies grow in appearance like withered trees
While their mouths spew forth intense flames
Which, streaming back onto them, scorch their bodies,
Giving them the appearance of burned *tāla* trees.

89 (T95)
When they go through the summer and wish for evening's coolness,
The light of the moon only increases the heat they feel.
When they abide in winter and long for daytime warmth,
Once the sunlight shines, it feels colder for them than ice.
When they move toward fruit on trees, it immediately disappears
And when they go to a river's waters, they straightaway all dry up.

90 (T96)
They live on for fifteen thousand years
Wherein karma preserves their lifespan, not allowing it to be cut off.
Their having to enduring for so long these countless sufferings
Is due to karmic offenses they committed in previous lives.

种种诸恼逼 纯苦初无间 贪惜极悭着 佛说饿鬼因	種種諸惱逼 純苦初無間 貪惜極慳著 佛說餓鬼因
生天虽快乐 福尽极大苦 斯非贤圣果 慧者所不怙	生天雖快樂 福盡極大苦 斯非賢聖果 慧者所不怙
身体不光泽 不乐本所座 华冠卒萎落 尘垢忽着身	身體不光澤 不樂本所座 華冠卒萎落 塵垢忽著身
腋下流汗汁 当知死时至 善趣净业尽 [17]复堕三恶道	腋下流汗汁 當知死時至 善趣淨業盡 [17]復墮三惡道
或生阿修罗 贪嫉常苦恼 虽有智聪明 终不见真谛	或生阿修羅 貪嫉常苦惱 雖有智聰明 終不見真諦
生死六趣中 轮转常不息 胜法不受生 生者众苦器	生死六趣中 輪轉常不息 勝法不受生 生者眾苦器
假令顶火然 正意慎勿念 不受后有业 专心[18]勤修习	假令頂火然 正意慎勿念 不受後有業 專心[18]勤修習
简体字	正體字

91 (T97)
They are driven along by all manner of afflictions,
Enduring absolute suffering, unremitting since its very onset.
The Buddha explained the cause for birth as a hungry ghost as being
Covetous cherishing involving the most extreme miserly attachment.

F. The Gods
92 (T98)
Although taking birth in the heavens is blissful,
Once merit has been exhausted, the most extreme sufferings ensue.
Hence this is not the karmic fruit sought by the Worthies and Āryas.
It is something on which the wise refuse to rely.

93 (T99)
The bodies of the gods lose their luster
And they are no longer happy where they formerly sat.
Their floral chaplets abruptly wilt and fall away
And filth suddenly begins to adhere to their bodies.

94 (T100-1)
When next their armpits begin to stream with perspiration,
One should realize then that the time of death has come.
When the pure karma which brought good rebirth is exhausted,
They plummet once again into the three wretched destinies.

G. The Asuras
95 (T102)
One may take rebirth as an *asura*, [a demigod],
Who is, [by nature], covetous, jealous, and afflicted with bitterness.
Although they may be possessed of sharp intelligence,
Still, to the very end, they remain incapable of perceiving the truths.[44]

H. Summation on Cyclic Existence
96 (T103)
In the six destinies of cyclic births and deaths,
One constantly turns about without cease.
The most supreme Dharma involves not being bound to take rebirths,
For those compelled to rebirth are receptacles of the many sufferings.

29. Exhortation to Pursue the Path with Vigor
97 (T104)
Just as, in an instance where flames burn [the turban] on one's head,
One acts with focused mind, being sure not to be lost in thought,
So too, in order to avoid creating karma compelling later existences,
One must [urgently] focus the mind on diligent cultivation.

简体字	正體字
戒品禅定慧 寂静调不动 [19]当求涅盘道 究竟离生死	戒品禪定慧 寂靜調不動 [19]當求涅槃道 究竟離生死
念择及精进 喜猗三昧舍 此七菩提分 清净甘露道	念擇及精進 喜猗三昧捨 此七菩提分 清淨甘露道
无智则不禅 无禅亦不智 是二俱成就 能出生死流 无边大苦海 视如牛迹水	無智則不禪 無禪亦不智 是二俱成就 能出生死流 無邊大苦海 視如牛跡水
十四无记论 佛说不应思 是非安隐道 亦非寂灭处	十四無記論 佛說不應思 是非安隱道 亦非寂滅處
无明缘诸行 即缘彼生识 名色从识起 六入因名色 六入生六触 从触起诸受	無明緣諸行 即緣彼生識 名色從識起 六入因名色 六入生六觸 從觸起諸受
诸受为爱因 从爱生四取 四取生三有 因有爱后生	諸受為愛因 從愛生四取 四取生三有 因有愛後生

30. Exhortation to Cultivate the Three Trainings and Seek Nirvāṇa
98 (T105)

It is through the moral precepts, dhyāna absorption, and wisdom
That one trains oneself in the unmoving state of quiescent stillness.
One must seek out the path to nirvāṇa
And proceed toward the ultimate abandonment of births and deaths.

31. The Seven Limbs of Enlightenment
99 (T106)

Mindfulness, dharmic analysis, vigor,
Joy, buoyant mental ease, samādhi, and equanimity—
These seven limbs of bodhi
Place one on the path to pure sweet-dew ambrosia (*amṛta*).[45]

32. The Necessity and Decisive Effect of Meditative Absorption and Wisdom
100 (T107)

In the absence of wisdom, one does not enter dhyāna absorption.
In the absence of dhyāna absorption, one is not wise, either.
If one is able to perfect both of these,
Then one is able to escape from the flow of birth and death
And, regarding the boundlessly great sea of suffering,
One sees it as a mere puddle in a bull's hoof print.

33. Avoidance of the Fourteen Indeterminate Dharmas
101 (T108)

The fourteen indeterminate theorizations[46]
Were declared by Buddha to be inappropriate for contemplation.
These are unrelated to the path of peace and security
And are not bases for achieving [nirvāṇa's] quiescent cessation.

34. The Twelve-Fold Chain of Causes and Conditions
102 (T109-10)

Ignorance serves as a condition for karmic actions.
Taking the "other" as its objective condition, it creates consciousness.
Name-and-form arises from consciousness
And the six sense faculties are in turn caused by name-and-form.[47]
The six sense faculties generate the six types of contact
And it is from contact that there is the production of all feeling.[48]

103

Feeling serves as a cause for craving
And it is from craving that the four types of grasping are produced.[49]
The four types of grasping produce the three realms of becoming
And it is on account of becoming that one craves subsequent births.[50]

简体字	正體字
从生致老死 忧悲诸苦恼 无量众苦聚 生尽[20]则[21]都灭	從生致老死 憂悲諸苦惱 無量眾苦聚 生盡[20]則[21]都滅
最胜所显示 甚深缘起法 若能正观察 真[22]实见之上 如是真实见 是则为见佛	最勝所顯示 甚深緣起法 若能正觀察 真[22]實見之上 如是真實見 是則為見佛
正见正思惟 正语正业命 正念正方便 及正三摩提 八分圣贤道 寂灭当修习	正見正思惟 正語正業命 正念正方便 及正三摩提 八分聖賢道 寂滅當修習
生为真谛苦 恩爱则是集 苦灭名解脱 到彼谓八道	生為真諦苦 恩愛則是集 苦滅名解脫 到彼謂八道
为见彼真谛 [23]常勤修正智 虽处五欲乐 慧者能出离	為見彼真諦 [23]常勤修正智 雖處五欲樂 慧者能出離
能证正法者 皆从凡夫起 不从虚空堕 亦不从地出	能證正法者 皆從凡夫起 不從虛空墮 亦不從地出

104 (T111)
It is from birth that there is the causation of ageing, death,
Worry, lamentation, and all manner of bitter affliction.
The mass of the innumerably many sufferings
Are all extinguished through the cessation of births.

105 (T112)
As for that which was revealed by the Supreme One
As the extremely profound dharma of conditioned arising,
If one were able to correctly contemplate and analyze it,
This in itself would be supreme among genuine perceptions.[51]
Just such a genuine perception as this
Amounts to seeing the Buddha.

35. The Eightfold Path
106 (T113)
Right views, right thought,
Right speech, right action and livelihood,
Right mindfulness, right effort,
And right samādhi—
These constitute the eightfold path of the Āryas and Worthies.
To realize [nirvāṇa's] quiescent cessation, one must cultivate them.

36. The Four Truths: Suffering, Accumulation, Cessation, and Path
107 (T114)
It is physical birth which makes for the "suffering" of the truths
And it is craving which is the source of "accumulation."
It is the "cessation" of suffering which qualifies as liberation.
That conducing to reaching that destination is the eightfold "path."[52]

III. Concluding Exhortatory Section
108 (T115)
For the sake of "seeing" those truths,
Be constant in the diligent cultivation guided by right knowledge.
Though one may dwell amidst of the pleasures of the five desires,
If one is wise, he will be able to succeed in abandoning them.

109 (T116)
Those who have been able to gain realization of right Dharma
All began as common persons.
They did not just drop down from empty space,
Nor did they simply grow forth from the earth.

明哲无畏王 领要不待烦 宜修正法桥 越度生死渊	明哲無畏王 領要不待煩 宜修正法橋 越度生死淵
如上诸深法 出家犹难精 况复御世主 而能具足行 随时渐修习 勿令日空过	如上諸深法 出家猶難精 況復御世主 而能具足行 隨時漸修習 勿令日空過
一切人修善 常生随喜心 自行三种业 正迴向佛道 当于未来世 受此无量福	一切人修善 常生隨喜心 自行三種業 正迴向佛道 當於未來世 受此無量福
常生天人中 得为自在王 与大菩萨众 游戏诸神通 方便化众生 严净佛国土	常生天人中 得為自在王 與大菩薩眾 遊戲諸神通 方便化眾生 嚴淨佛國土
施戒慧为种 往返人天中 无垢净名称 流布十方国	施戒慧為種 往返人天中 無垢淨名稱 流布十方國
世间导人主 上生化天王 令舍五欲乐 远离诸放逸	世間導人主 上生化天王 令捨五欲樂 遠離諸放逸
简体字	正體字

Chapter 2: *The Saṅghavarman Suhṛllekha Translation*

110 (T117)
The sagacious and fearless king
Grasps the essentials and doesn't tarry in troublesome complexities.
It is fitting that one cultivate the bridge of right Dharma
And thus cross beyond the abyss of births and deaths.

111 (T118)
Profound dharmas such as set forth above
Would be difficult to perfect even for a monastic.
How much the less might a world-ruling lord
Be able to practice them completely.
One may gradually cultivate them as time allows.
Still, one must not allow one's days to pass emptily by.

112 (T119)
When any person at all cultivates goodness,
Always bring forth thoughts of joyful accordance with it.
The three types of karmic actions which one cultivates
Should be directly dedicated to realization of the Buddha Path.[53]
Thus, in a future life, one will be able
To receive [the fruits of] this incalculably vast merit.

113 (T120-1)
Constantly take on birth among gods and humans,
Becoming for them a sovereignly-independent king.
Acting in concert with the congregation of great bodhisattvas,
Roam about, bringing into play the spiritual superknowledges.
Use skillful means to carry on the transformative teaching of beings,
And, in so doing, adorn and purify the buddhaland.

114 (T122-23)
Disseminating giving, moral virtue, and wisdom like seeds,
Travel back and forth among humans and gods,
Making the stainless purity of their illustriousness
Spread throughout the lands of the ten directions.

115
When in the World, serve as a ruler acting as the people's guide.
Above, take births as kings bringing transformative teaching to gods.
Influence them then to relinquish the pleasures of the five desires
And to abandon all endeavors neglectful [of the Path].

众生迷正济
漂浪随四流
无量生死苦
度令至彼岸
缘此成佛道
究竟大涅盘

劝发诸王要偈

简体字

眾生迷正濟
漂浪隨四流
無量生死苦
度令至彼岸
緣此成佛道
究竟大涅槃

勸發諸王要偈

正體字

116

Beings abide in confusion about the right means to be rescued
And so are swept along in the waves of the four floods.[54]
They endure countless sufferings amidst cyclic births and deaths.
Bring them across to liberation, causing them to reach that far shore.
Taking this as the goal, gain realization of the path to buddhahood,
Realizing as well the ultimate great nirvāṇa.[55]

The Dharma Essentials Verses for the Exhortation of Kings

(The end of the Tripiṭaka Master Saṅghavarman translation.)

Endnotes to the Saṅghavarman Edition

1. As noted in the introduction to this volume, although the king in question here may indeed have been a "friend" of Nāgārjuna in the loose sense of the term, it is Nāgārjuna who adopts in this letter of instruction the role of the "good spiritual friend" (*kalyāṇa-mitra*) or "spiritual guide" and it is for that reason I render the Sanskrit title, *Suhṛllekha*, as "Letter *from* a Friend," and not as "Letter *to* a Friend" (as has been the case with most of the English translations originating with the Tibetan). Indeed, it is Nāgārjuna who is the ārya, not the King. Only an ārya can be relied upon to be one's friend in this and all future lives. The king, "friend" that he might be for the time being, might just as easily change into a deadly enemy with a change of circumstances (say, were he to convert to another religions, for instance) or a change of lifetimes. I suppose it should be noted that there is nothing in the Sanskrit title which defines it as intending either "from" or "to." Restricting it to one interpretation or the other is an artifact of having to produce a rendering into English.
2. The "brahman voice" (*brahma-svara*) is one of the thirty-two major marks of the Buddha. It is characterized by a number of marvelous qualities not found in any human voice.
3. Emending the text (substituting 月 for 日) to correct an obvious scribal error whereby the character for "sun" had erroneously been used in place of the character for "moon" which is attested by the two other Chinese editions and the Tibetan as well.
4. The "Three Jewels" are the Buddha, the Dharma, and the Ārya Sangha.
5. N makes it clear elsewhere (In *Mppu*, in his discussion of the recollections) that this refers not just to "giving," but also to the "giving up" or "relinquishing" of the afflictions.
6. "The Victorious One" is another name for the Buddha.
7. The "recollections" vary in the number of components taught. For example, in *Mppu*, N explains that sutra's list of "eight recollections" which, in addition to these six, includes "the breath," and "death." See my translation of *Nāgārjuna on the Eight Recollections*.
8. "Skillful reality-based contemplation" probably occurs in this text especially in regard to mindfulness of "the heavens," this because, although the heavens are indeed the effect brought about by the ten good deeds, they are nonetheless impermanent, too blissful to inspire

creation of much additional good karma or cultivation of the Path, and are bound to result in one's plunging back into the cycle of endless suffering. Hence they are not a desired endpoint for any of the Buddhist paths. On the contrary, they are potentially a trap. That said, they may be used to encourage cultivation of good karma and abandonment of bad karma in individuals who cannot bring themselves to cultivate the Path and who would otherwise continue to course in disastrously negative karma.

9. The ten good karmic deeds involve abstention from: killing, stealing, sexual misconduct (the three of the body), lying, harsh speech, divisive speech, lewd or frivolous speech (the four of the mouth), covetousness, hatefulness, and wrong views (the three of the mind). N elsewhere (in his commentary on the ten bodhisattva grounds) holds forth on the path of the ten good karmic deeds at great length, pointing that they are the basis for the realization of all of the fruits of the Buddhist paths up to and including buddhahood.

10. In his *Mppu*, N identifies the five parties destined to become beneficiaries of one's wealth as: the king, thieves, fire, floods, and unloving sons (T25.1509.156c).

11. "Field" here refers to a "field of merit," a standard concept in all Buddhist traditions. "Field of merit" is a metaphoric reference to the fact that making gifts to others, particularly those of highly-evolved spiritual station, is, karmically-speaking, like planting seeds of merit in a fertile field (the most fertile being a buddha). These are bound to "sprout" and bear fruit in this and later lives as fortunate karmic outcomes involving easy acquisition of wealth, long life, and so forth.

12. "Three realms of existence" is a reference to the desire realm, form realm, and formless realm which in turn contain within them roughly thirty stations of existence ranging from the hells at the bottom of the desire realm on up through the stations of hungry ghosts, animals, humans, the six desire-realm heavens, sixteen form-realm heavens corresponding to the four dhyānas, and four formless realm heavens corresponding to the formless absorptions of limitless space, limitless consciousness, nothing whatsoever, and the station of neither perception nor non-perception.

13. Lest it not be obvious, this is a reference to becoming a fully-enlightened buddha. A *"muni"* is a general reference to recluses devoted usually to meditation and often to silence as well.

14. Obviously, sexual relations within the bounds of marriage is not proscribed for householders. The reference here is to short-term voluntary training for lay people through the skillful means of taking the eight precepts, usually only for single day or, alternately for six set

days each month.

15. "The other three transgressing factors" is a reference to: 1) perfume or makeup, music or dancing or going to performances of same; 2) indulging a fondness for high or wide seats or beds; 3) eating past the noon hour, strictly interpreted as noon straight up.

16. Emending the obvious scribal error (斉) with the clearly intended character (齋). These eight precepts constitute the layperson's training regimen in the observance of enhanced moral virtue. They are commonly observed according to three different patterns, this after formally accepting them in a bhikshu-administered ceremony: for one day only, from the first to the fifteenth day of the twelfth lunar month, or, in the more standard form known as the *upavāsa*, on the eighth, fourteenth, fifteenth, twenty-third, twenty-ninth, and thirtieth days of each lunar month. See my translation of *Nāgārjuna on the Perfection of Moral Virtue* for a more extended discussion of all of the specifics involved in the eight-precepts *upavāsa*.

17. "Non-returner" refers specifically to third-stage arhatship.

18. This is a reference to grain-derived sweeteners such as maltose.

19. The *bimba* fruit (identified by the Monier-Williams as *Momordica Monadelpha*) is a common comparison in traditional Sanskrit literature for beautiful ruby-red lips. The much-later Yijing and Tibetan editions refer to the *kimpāka* fruit which is outwardly attractive and sweet-tasting, but which nonetheless contains a deadly poisonous interior. (The Guṇavarman translation uses neither analogy.)

20. Although the literal meaning of the Chinese characters (不淨) is in fact "impurity," that is oftentimes a mere "stock" translation adopted by Sino-Buddhism for the Sanskrit *aśubha* which means "unlovely." In the absence of any proof of the actual Sanskrit antecedents here, it doesn't hurt to employ both concepts in the contemplation. Contemplation of the thirty-two (or thirty-six) parts of the body or of the nine stages of a corpse's deterioration makes both ideas abundantly clear.

21. It's common to interpret this common Buddhist analogy as pointing to leprosy, but leprosy is not marked by itching as a cardinal symptom. Also, it is caused by bacteria, not by parasitic mites. The Chinese characters used to translate the Sanskrit in all three editions indicate "scabies" which does indeed involve extreme itching created by the boring of the scabies mite and the ensuing allergic reaction.

22. In his *Ratnāvalī* (*Strand of Jewels*), Nāgārjuna makes this idea clearer still:
    0497a17: 如搔癢謂樂不癢最安樂
    0497a18: 如此有欲樂無欲人最樂
    Just as scratching an itch might be thought pleasurable,

> When having no itch is most pleasant of all,
> So too it is with pleasures linked to desire,
> For those free of desire are the happiest of all.
> (寶行王正論 / T25.1656.497a17-8)

23. Nāgārjuna is in no way suggesting that the King should dispense with other recommended practices for accumulating merit and wisdom. He is merely pointing to the superior potency of analytic contemplation in defeating delusions (such as the lust-based attachments just discussed) and in fathoming the ultimate reality of any given phenomenon.

24. "The seven valuables of the Āryas" (ārya-dhana) is a commonly encountered list in both the Āgamas and Mahāyāna Sutras.

25. Adopting the variant (天) found in three other editions of the text and also in all three other translations of the text (GV, YJ, T), this to correct an obvious and easily made scribal error (大).

26. These four mind-training states are known as the "four immeasurable minds" (apramāṇa-citta) and are also referred to as the "four abodes of Brahmā" (brahma-vihāra). For an extensive discussion of this topic and the differences in their cultivation by individual-liberation and universal-liberation practitioners, see my translation of *Nāgārjuna on the Four Immeasurable Minds* under separate cover.

27. Of course rebirth in the heavens is considered to be extremely problematic in Buddhism, this because it only serves to keep one trapped in uncontrolled cyclic births and deaths. Hence it is recommended that one invoke the resolve to follow the path to the Path and instead dedicate all merit to that higher goal which might otherwise conduce to celestial rebirth. This would be equally true of individual-liberation vehicle practitioners and universal-liberation vehicle practitioners.

28. No inverse articulation of the "salt-in-water" analogy is found in any of the other editions of the text, this independent of the SV text's very apt introduction here of "poison" in place of salt. This may well represent a commentarial interpolation. We have no clue as to whether it is of Indian or Chinese origin.

29. The Yijing and Tibetan editions refer specifically to the five hindrances as the "thieves" in this śloka. GV refers to "five erroneous courses of conduct" (五邪). This SV edition's comparison of the five aggregates to thieves is not uncommon in the Canon and so is not particularly idiosyncratic.

30. The five root-faculties are faith, vigor, mindfulness, concentration, and wisdom. When they become completely developed, they are then referred to as the five powers.

31. My bracketed "and so forth" is intended to indicate that the entire

list of the eight sufferings is intended to be inferred. They are: birth, aging, sickness, death, estrangement from the loved, proximity to what is hated, inability to gain what one seeks, the suffering inherent in the five aggregates. The GV edition refers specifically to "the eight sufferings."

32. This SV edition is somewhat cryptic in its description of the four wrong views about the relationship of the form aggregate to the existence of a self and assumes the reader will infer the more complete description. The GV edition spells them all out quite clearly: "…form is not self, self is not form, / There is no form to be found within a self, and there is no self to be found within form—." (T32.1672.746b)

33. The text recites here a short list of wrong views on the origins of the phenomena upon which "self" is imputed, then concludes with the most crucial three of the twelve causal links figuring in the perpetuation of a seeming karmic continuity. SV translates the name of the Iśvara god into Chinese which, if translated in turn into English, would produce the clumsy and distracting "the god Sovereignly Independent" or some such. Hence I simply reconstruct the Sanskrit. Although "aggregates" are not specified in the text, that they are intended is obvious from the previous śloka. Hence I insert them in brackets.

34. Emending the text to correct a scribal error by substituting "truths" (*di* - 諦) for "dhyāna" (*chan* - 禪), based on issues of sensibility and also on the fact that none of the other three editions make any mention of the four dhyānas here and all three of them refer explicitly to the four truths. The corruption could have occurred relatively easily in calligraphic transmittal of texts.

An additional point upon which this emendation is based is that the topic being treated is "liberation." In all schools of Buddhism, liberation is inextricably connected with realization of the four truths. In no traditional school of Buddhism can it be validly stated that the four dhyānas have anything but a facilitating role in the achievement of liberation. To quote the Venerable Master Hsuan Hua: "The four dhyānas are only preliminary exercises, that's all." (Quoted from unpublished meditation-session instructional talks.)

35. This analogy originates with the Buddha. There is but one blind turtle and it rises to the surface of the ocean but once every hundred years. There is only one yoke floating randomly around on the world's oceans. The turtle happens to poke its head up in just the right way that it is as if harnessed in it. This describes the difficulty of regaining human rebirth having once fallen down into the realm of animals.

36. The "good spiritual friend" (*kalyāṇa-mitra*) is in most cases an artful term of reference for one's guru or "spiritual guide."

37. From the *Dīrgha-āgama Sutra*: "What are the four dharmas of success? They are what are referred to as "the four wheels." The first is residence in a central land. The second is proximity to the good spiritual friend. The third is being diligently careful [as regards one's karmic actions]. The fourth is having planted the roots of goodness in previous lives." (T01.0001.53b)
38. "Brahmin conduct" (*brahma-carya*) explicitly refers to strict celibacy.
39. "Quiescent cessation" is a Chinese translation of the Sanskrit *nirvāṇa*.
40. Abiding in the long-life heavens involves a complete absence of motivation to cultivate the path of liberation and typically results in a plummeting into the wretched destinies once the celestial lifespan comes to an end, this because one's merit has become completely exhausted. This is comparable to spending all of one's savings at an expensive resort, thus sentencing oneself thereafter to the life of a beggar living in a bad neighborhood.
41. The eight difficulties: birth in the hells; birth among the hungry ghosts, birth among the animals, birth on the continent of Uttarakuru (a blissful place largely free of sufferings, but lacking in Dharma); birth in the long-life heavens (of the form and formless realm); being afflicted with blindness, deafness, or muteness; being possessed of a contentious intelligence which bases itself solely in worldly knowledge (thus making oneself a philistine with respect to spiritual priorities).
42. The YJ and Tibetan clearly reference resilience of the celestial grounds upon which one walks. It would not be so easy to extract that meaning here where the reference seems to be to ascent and descent on Mount Sumeru occurring in response to the druthers of one's ideation. It's also possible that the intended concept is that one's karmic rise and fall adapts to the quality of one's mental life (i.e. the relative purity or impurity of thought). There is no specific mention of this in the GV edition which varies markedly from all others in this section.
43. "Non-Intermittent Hells" is a Chinese translation for the Avīci Hells.
44. "Truths" here is a reference to the four truths (suffering, its origination, its cessation, the path to its cessation), the direct perception of which is key to realization of the fruits of all Buddhist Paths.
45. "Sweet-dew ambrosia (*amṛta*)" is synonymous with nirvāṇa and deathlessness.

Perhaps one should be aware that the seven limbs of bodhi vary somewhat from text to text in the way they are listed. Basically, they are: dharmic analysis, vigor, joy, buoyant mental ease (*praśrabdhi*), mindfulness, concentration, and, depending on the scripture, either "wisdom," or the "equanimity" associated with the formative-factor aggregate (as opposed to the equanimity with regard to the "feelings" aggregate which is so important in the acquisition of the dhyānas). The role of formative-factor equanimity in wisdom should be fairly obvious, however. Hence the difference between the two lists is relatively insignificant.

46. The fourteen are: Are the World and the self eternal, non-eternal, both, or neither?; Do the World and the self come to an end, or not, or both, or neither?; Does the Buddha continue to exist after his nirvāṇa, or not, or both, or neither?; Are the body and the soul identical or different? The Buddha deemed that answering these questions would serve no purpose, not least because they were like asking, "How much milk can one obtain from a bull's horn?" and hence would not conduce toward awakening.
47. "Name-and-form" is a term referencing the mental ("name") and physical ("form") aggregates upon which personhood is typically imputed.
48. "Feeling" is of six types corresponding to the six sense faculties. It is often misconstrued as referencing just physical sensation or just emotional "feelings." In fact it refers to both. Vasubandhu makes this quite clear in his *Abhidharma-kośa-bāṣyam*.
49. The four types of grasping: grasping at [objects of] desire; grasping at views; grasping at mistaken conceptions of what constitutes moral virtue; grasping at a "self."
50. "The three realms of becoming" refers to existence in the desire realm, in the form realm, and in the formless realm.
51. "Supreme One" is a direct reference to the Buddha himself.
52. One will notice that the simple logic behind the four truths is described in this śloka, wherein the "craving" link in the twelve-fold causal chain is indicated as at the same time key to the generation of suffering and also key to its cessation.
53. The "three types of karmic actions" refers to one's own actions of body, mouth, and mind.
54. The four floods (*catur-ogha*) are views (*dṛṣṭi-ogha*), desire (*kāma-ogha*), "becoming / existence" (*bhava-ogha*), and ignorance (*avidyā-ogha*).
55. For the bodhisattva and buddha, nirvāṇa is realized as the constant state of affairs in every moment and thus does not entail abandonment of continued work for the spiritual liberation of beings.

Letter From a Friend (The *Suhṛllekha*)
Edition Three: The Yijing Translation

*Nāgārjuna Bodhisattva's Verses
Exhorting and Admonishing the King*

Translated by the Tripiṭaka Master Yijing
Of the Great Tang Dynasty (circa 673 CE)

English Translation by Bhikshu Dharmamitra

龙树菩萨劝诫王颂

[1]大唐三藏法师义净译

此颂是龙树菩萨以诗代书。寄与南印度亲友乘[2]土国王一首。此书已先译神州处藏人多不见。遂令妙语不得详知。为此更定本文。冀使流通罔滞。沙门义净创至东印度耽摩立底国译

　　有情无知覆心故
　　由此兴悲为开解
　　大德龙树为国王
　　寄书与彼令修学

此一行颂乃是后人所述标书本意也

　　具德我演如如教
　　为生福[3]爱而兴述
　　真善宜应可审听
　　此颂名为圣只底

　　随何木等雕佛像
　　诸有智者咸供养
　　纵使我诗非巧妙
　　依正法说勿当轻

LETTER FROM A FRIEND[1]

Nāgārjuna Bodhisattva's Verses
Exhorting and Admonishing the King

Translated by the Tang Dynasty Tripiṭaka Master Yijing

These verses are a poetic work presented as a letter by Nāgārjuna Bodhisattva to a close friend, the king of the South Indian country of *Chengtu*.[2] This "letter" was already translated at an earlier time. Nonetheless, it has for the most part not been seen by those who peruse the Canon in Shenzhou. The result has been that it has been impossible to gain a detailed knowledge of these marvelous words. On account of this, there has now been an additional publication of the original text, this with the hope that it might be caused to circulate unimpededly. This work was translated by Śramaṇa Yijing when he journeyed to the Eastern Indian state of Amaravati.[3]

I. INTRODUCTION AND ENCOURAGEMENT TO PAY DUE ATTENTION

1

Because ignorance covers over the minds of beings,
May compassion flourish from this so they begin to comprehend.[4]
"The greatly virtuous eminence Nāgārjuna, for the sake of the King,
Sent this letter to him to influence him to cultivate and study it."[5]

> **An editorial note added to the Chinese comments on the above line:**
> "This one stanza line was written by some later person to indicate the basic rationale for composing the letter."

2   (T1)

Meritorious One, I expound the authentic teaching
And let flourish this writing in order to generate fondness for merit.
The truly good will find it appropriate to listen studiously.
These verses describe the grand foundation of the Āryas' intent.

3   (T2)

Whichever wood or other material is used to sculpt a buddha image,
The wise are all inspired by it to make offerings.
Even if my verses are not artful or sublime,
Do not slight them, for they rely on proclamations of right Dharma.

| 简体字 | 正體字 |

王虽先解如如教
更闻佛语增胜解
犹如粉壁月光辉
岂不鲜明益姝妙

佛法并僧众
施戒及与天
一一功德聚
佛说应常念

十善诸业道
身语意常亲
远离于诸酒
亦行清净命

知财体非固
如法施苾刍
贫贱及再生
来世为亲友

众德依戒住
如地长一切
勿宂瘦杂[4]悕
佛说应常习

施戒忍勇定
惠不可称量
此能到应修
渡有海成佛

若孝养父母
其家有梵王
现招善名称
来世生天堂

——

王雖先解如如教
更聞佛語增勝解
猶如粉壁月光輝
豈不鮮明益姝妙

佛法並僧眾
施戒及與天
一一功德聚
佛說應常念

十善諸業道
身語意常親
遠離於諸酒
亦行清淨命

知財體非固
如法施苾芻
貧賤及再生
來世為親友

眾德依戒住
如地長一切
勿宂瘦雜[4]悕
佛說應常習

施戒忍勇定
惠不可稱量
此能到應修
渡有海成佛

若孝養父母
其家有梵王
現招善名稱
來世生天堂

4 (T3)
Though the King may have already understood authentic teachings,
Listening to Buddha's words again refines supreme comprehension,
Just as when a plaster wall is seen in the radiance of the moonlight—
How could its fresh brilliance not appear especially sublime?

II. THE MAIN DOCTRINAL SECTION
01. THE SIX RECOLLECTIONS

5 (T4)
[Recollection of] the Buddha, the Dharma, the Sangha,
Giving,⁶ moral virtue, and the heavens—
These are bases for collecting each and every meritorious quality,
The Buddha declared that one should always bear them in mind.⁷

02. THE TEN GOOD DEEDS, ABANDONMENT OF INTOXICANTS, RIGHT LIVELIHOOD

6 (T5)
As for the path of the ten good karmic deeds,⁸
One should constantly draw close to them in body, speech, and mind.
Abandon all forms of intoxicants
While also practicing pure livelihood.

03. THE SIX PERFECTIONS

7 (T6)
Realize that wealth and the body are not durable.
In accordance with Dharma, practice giving to the Bhikshus,
To the poor, to the lowly, and also to the "born-again" (*dvija*).⁹
That [this giving] may become your close friend in future lives.¹⁰

8 (T7)
The manifold virtues abide in reliance on the precepts
Just as all things grow forth from the earth.
Do not indulge, but rather reduce the various aspirations.
Buddha declared this as something one should constantly practice.

9 (T8)
As for giving, moral virtue, patience, vigor, meditative discipline,
And immeasurably-vast wisdom,
These enable reaching one's destination and so should be cultivated
In order to cross beyond the sea of existences and become a buddha.¹¹

04. FILIAL RESPECT FOR PARENTS

10 (T9)
If one cares for one's parents with filial attentiveness,
His own household will be attended by the Brahma Heaven King.
In the present, he will elicit a fine reputation.
In the future life, he will be born into celestial palaces.

简体字	正體字
杀盗婬妄[5]说 耽食爱高床 断诸酒歌舞 华彩及涂香	殺盜婬妄[5]說 耽食愛高床 斷諸酒歌舞 華彩及塗香
若女男能成 此八支圣戒 欲界六天上 长净善当生	若女男能成 此八支聖戒 欲界六天上 長淨善當生
悭谄诳贪怠 慢婬嗔氏族 多闻年少娇 并视如怨贼	慳諂誑貪怠 慢婬嗔氏族 多聞年少嬌 並視如怨賊
说无生由勤 有死因放逸 勤能长善法 尔可修谨慎	說無生由勤 有死因放逸 勤能長善法 爾可修謹慎
先时离放逸 后若改勤修 犹如云翳除 良[6]宵觏明月	先時離放逸 後若改勤修 猶如雲翳除 良[6]宵覩明月
孙陀罗难陀 [7]央具理摩罗 达[8]舍绮莫迦 翻恶皆成善	孫陀羅難陀 [7]央具理摩羅 達[8]舍綺莫迦 翻惡皆成善
勇进无同忍 勿使忿势行 终得不还位 佛证可除嗔	勇進無同忍 勿使忿勢行 終得不還位 佛證可除嗔

Chapter 3: *The Yijing Suhṛllekha Translation*

05. The Layperson's Eight-Precept *Upavāsa* Abstinence Rite

11 (T10)
Abstinence from killing, stealing, sexual relations,[12] false speech,
Indulgence in untimely eating, fondness for high seats and beds—
Cutting off all intoxicants, singing, dancing,
Floral adornment, cosmetics, and perfumes—

12 (T11)
If either women or men are able to perfectly observe
These eight moral precepts of the Āryas,[13]
Then, among the six heavens of the desire realm,
They will be reborn in the abode of enduring purity and goodness.

06. Abandonment of Faults

13 (T12)
Miserliness, flattery, deceptiveness, covetousness, indolence,
Pride, lust, hatred, caste-based arrogance, clan-based arrogance,
And arrogance based on extensive learning or youthful qualities—
All of these should be looked upon as enemies.

07. Diligence versus Negligence

14 (T13)
[Buddha] stated that realizing the unproduced arises from diligence
And that vulnerability to death is caused by negligence in cultivation.
Diligence is able to bring about the growth of good dharmas,
Hence you could cultivate with scrupulous carefulness.[14]

15 (T14)
If one abandons neglectfulness of the past
And changes, cultivating diligently henceforth,
This is comparable to when obscuring clouds are pushed aside
And, on a lovely night, one gazes up at the brilliant moon.

16
Sundarananda,[15]
Aṅgulimāla,[16]
And Kṣemadarśin[17]
All turned away from evil and perfected goodness.

08. On the Special Importance of Patience and Relinquishing Enmity

17 (T15)
In making valiant progress, nothing is the equal of patience.
One must not allow the power of anger to manifest in one's actions.
Then, finally, one will gain the station of the "non-returner."[18]
Buddha verified that [patience] enables riddance of hatefulness.

简体字	正體字
他人打骂我 欺陵夺我财 怀恨招怨诤 舍恨眠安乐	他人打罵我 欺陵奪我財 懷恨招怨諍 捨恨眠安樂
[9]如于水土石 人心尽彼同 起烦恼前胜 爱法者如后	[9]如於水土石 人心盡彼同 起煩惱前勝 愛法者如後
佛说三种语 人美实虚言 犹如蜜花粪 弃后可行前	佛說三種語 人美實虛言 猶如蜜花糞 棄後可行前
今明后亦明 今暗后还暗 或今明后暗 或今暗后明 如是四种人 王当依第一	今明後亦明 今闇後還闇 或今明後闇 或今闇後明 如是四種人 王當依第一
自有生如熟 亦有熟如生 亦有熟如熟 或复生如生	自有生如熟 亦有熟如生 亦有熟如熟 或復生如生
菴没罗果中 有如是差别 人亦同彼四 难识王应知	菴沒羅果中 有如是差別 人亦同彼四 難識王應知

18 (T16)

"That person struck me, scolded me,
Cheated me, persecuted me, stole my wealth...."
Such nursing of grudges brings on the feuding of enemies.
When one lets go of grudges, one sleeps peacefully.

19 (T17)

Just as when drawing on water, inscribing in dirt, or carving stone—
Just so may be the effect of one's mental actions.
In the arising of afflictions, the former is the best.
In cherishing Dharma, one prefers the latter.

09. Three Kinds of Discourse
20 (T18)

The Buddha stated that there are three types of discourse:
Words which please people, true words, and false words.
Accordingly, they are like honey, like flowers, or like feces.
Cast out the latter while putting to use the previous types.

10. Criteria for Evaluating Both Self and Prospective Associates
A. Four Types of Personal Destinies Linked to Brilliance or Darkness
21 (T19)

People may now abide in brilliance and be brilliant later as well,
May now abide in darkness and later still abide in darkness,
May now abide in brilliance, but later abide in darkness,
Or may now abide in darkness, but later abide in brilliance.
Of these four sorts of persons,
The King should be reliant on the first.

B. Four Types of Persons Compared to a Mango's Ripeness
22 (T20)

There are [mangoes] which are unripe but which appear to be ripe,
Those which are ripe but which appear to be unripe,
Those which are ripe and also appear to be ripe,
And those which are still unripe and also appear to be unripe.

23

Among the fruits of the mango,
There are distinctions such as these.
People, too, are the same as those four types.
The King should be aware that they may be difficult to distinguish.

简体字	正體字
勿觀他妻室 设观如母女 姊妹想随年 起贪思不净	勿覷他妻室 設觀如母女 姊妹想隨年 起貪思不淨
如闻子藏命 防持躁动心 兽药[10]刀怨火 无令欲乐侵	如聞子藏命 防持躁動心 獸藥[10]刀怨火 無令欲樂侵
由欲作无利 譬如兼博果 佛说彼应除 生死牢枷锁	由欲作無利 譬如兼博果 佛說彼應除 生死牢枷鎖
谲诳常摇境 能[1]降斯六识 执[2]仗扫众怨 许初为勇极	譎誑常搖境 能[1]降斯六識 執[2]仗掃眾怨 許初為勇極
臭气九门众秽室 行躯难满薄皮缠 请看少女除庄彩 折别形骸恶叵言	臭氣九門眾穢室 行軀難滿薄皮纏 請看少女除莊彩 折別形骸惡叵言
癞虫穿已痛 求安就火边 [3]止息无由[4]免 耽欲亦同然	癩虫穿已痛 求安就火邊 [3]止息無由[4]免 耽欲亦同然
为知真胜理 作意观众事 唯斯德应习 无馀法可亲	為知真勝理 作意觀眾事 唯斯德應習 無餘法可親

11. On Dealing with Desire
A. On Guarding the Mind

24 (T21)

Don't let your gaze fall on the wife or consort of another man.
If it should happen, contemplate her as one's own mother, daughter,
Or sister, reflecting as befits her age.
If lust arises, deliberate upon impurity.[19]

25 (T22)

Just as with one's reputation, one's son, one's valuables, or one's life,
Guard against and restrain any restive movement by the mind.
Just as one guards against beasts, poison, blades, enemies, or fire,
So too, prevent lust from invading.

B. On the Hazards Inherent in Desire

26 (T23)

Through desire, one becomes involved with what is so non-beneficial
As to be likened to the [attractive, but poisonous] *kimpāka* fruit.[20]
The Buddha declared that one should cast off
The manacles and fetters of birth-and-death's prison.

C. On the Superior Valor in Controlling Desire

27 (T24)

In comparing one beset by the deceptive, ever-harassing sense realms
Who is able to subdue these six sense consciousnesses
With someone else taking up arms to drive away a host of enemies,
We must acknowledge the first as the ultimate in valor.

D. On the Impurity of the Body

28 (T25)

A foul-smelling chamber exuding many sorts of filth from nine gates,
This moving carcass, so hard to keep filled, is encased by a thin skin.
Please, observe a young woman bereft of adornments or cosmetics.
Body parts and bones, considered apart, are unspeakably repulsive.

29 (T26)

When the boring of itch-inducing parasites becomes painful,
One may draw close to fire, seeking relief.[21]
But once one ceases that, there is no way to avoid [pain's return].
Indulgence in the desires is just the same as this.[22]

12. In Praise of Contemplation-Based Insight, Wisdom, and Moral Virtue

30 (T27)

For the sake of knowing the genuine and supreme reality,
One may analytically contemplate a multitude of phenomena.
[To gain such insight], one need only practice this meritorious skill,
For there are no other dharmas which can approach it.[23]

简体字	正體字
若人具族望 貌美复多闻 无智破尸罗 是人何足[5]责	若人具族望 貌美復多聞 無智破尸羅 是人何足[5]（責）［貴］
若人无族望 貌丑寡知闻 有智护尸罗 人皆应供养	若人無族望 貌醜寡知聞 有智護尸羅 人皆應供養
利无利苦乐 称无称毁讥 了俗世八法 齐心离斯境	利無利苦樂 稱無稱毀（譏）［譽］ 了俗世八法 齊心離斯境
再生天乞士 父母妻子人 勿由斯造罪 狱果他不分	再生天乞士 父母妻子人 勿由斯造罪 獄果他不分
若行诸罪业 非如刀斩伤 待至临终际 恶业果全彰	若行諸罪業 非如刀斬傷 待至臨終際 惡業果全彰
信戒施净闻 惭愧及正慧 七财牟尼说 共有物诚虚	信戒施淨聞 慚愧及正慧 七財牟尼說 共有物誠虛
博弈乐观喧杂境 嬾惰恶友敦亲志 饮酒非时行六过 此劫芳名尔应弃	博弈樂觀諠雜境 嬾惰惡友敦親志 飲酒非時行六過 此劫芳名爾應棄

31 (T28)
Where someone is of prestigious social caste
And possesses a pleasing appearance and abundant learning,
But has no wisdom and breaks śīla's moral prohibitions,
How is such a person worthy of esteem?[24]

32
If a person is not of prestigious social caste,
Has a homely appearance, and has but little experience or learning,
But possesses wisdom and guards against breaking śīla's moral code,
He is thereby worthy of offerings from everyone.

13. On Avoiding the Eight Worldly Dharmas and Offenses Inspired by Others
33 (T29)
Gain and loss, happiness and suffering,
Esteem and disgrace, praise and blame—[25]
Completely comprehend these eight worldly dharmas,
And, imposing order on one's thoughts, abandon these mind states.

34 (T30)
As for members of the "born-again" caste, gods, almsmen,
One's father, mother, wife, sons, or others,
Do not create karmic offenses on their account,
For they will not share with you the karmic retributions in hell.

14. On the Delayed Arrival of Karmic Retributions
35 (T31)
If one commits some karmic deed entailing retribution,
It does not manifest straightaway like a wound inflicted by a sword.
Rather it waits until one is close to the moment of death.
Then the retributions for evil karmic deeds will be entirely revealed.

15. On the Āryas' Seven Forms of Wealth
36 (T32)
Faith, moral virtue, giving, pure learning,
A sense of shame, a dread of blame, and right wisdom
Are the seven forms of wealth [of the Āryas] spoken of by the Muni.[26]
Things commonly possessed [as wealth] are actually mere vanities.

16. On Six Coarse Faults to Be Eliminated
37 (T33)
Gambling, attending clamorous or unseemly entertainments,
Indolence, consorting with bad friends,
Intoxication, and going out at inappropriate times, these six faults—
These steal away a fine reputation and so should be done away with.

简体字	正體字
求财少欲最 人天师盛陈 [6]若能修少欲 虽贫是富人	求財少欲最 人天師盛陳 [6]若能修少欲 雖貧是富人
若人广求诸事者 还被尔许苦来加 智者若不修少欲 受恼还如众首蛇	若人廣求諸事者 還被爾許苦來加 智者若不修少欲 受惱還如眾首蛇
禀性抱怨如杀者 欺轻夫主如[7]男偶 纵使片物必行偷 宜可弃兹三贼妇	稟性抱怨如殺者 欺輕夫主如[7]男偶 縱使片物必行偷 宜可棄茲三賊婦
顺若姊妹慈如母 随从若婢伴犹亲 如兹四妇宜应供 应知此室号天人	順若姊妹慈如母 隨從若婢伴猶親 如茲四婦宜應供 應知此室號天人
受飡如服药 知量去贪嗔 不为肥憍傲 但欲[8]住持身	受飡如服藥 知量去貪嗔 不為肥憍傲 但欲[8]住持身
勤躯度永日 于初后夜中 眠梦犹存念 勿使命虚终	勤軀度永日 於初後夜中 眠夢猶存念 勿使命虛終
慈悲喜正舍 [9]修习可常研 上流虽未入 能生梵世天	慈悲喜正捨 [9]修習可常研 上流雖未入 能生梵世天

17. In Praise of Reduced Desires

38 (T34)
Having but few desires is the best form of wealth.
This was extensively taught by the Teacher of Gods and Men.²⁷
If one is able to cultivate having but few desires,
Then, even though poor, he is in fact a rich man.

39 (T35)
If one extensively seeks all manner of things,
He is paradoxically beset by just that many sorts of sufferings.
The wise realize that, if one fails to cultivate having but few desires,
Like the many-headed dragon, he falls prey to [yet more] aggravation.

18. On the Various Sorts of Candidates for Marriage

40 (T36)
One naturally inclined to be as resentful as an assassin,
One deceiving and slighting her husband, treating him like a puppet,
Or one compelled to steal even trivial things—
It is fitting to reject these three insurgent-like women as a wife.

41 (T37)
One as accommodating as a sister, one as lovingly-kind as a mother,
One compliant as a servant, or as companionate as a close relative—
Any of these four potential wives are worthy of your gifts.
One should realize such a wife is fit to be addressed as a goddess.

19. On Moderation and Sensibility in Eating

42 (T38)
One should take one's meals as if ingesting medicine,
Being aware of right measure and being rid of craving and aversion.
One does not eat to enhance [connoisseurial] pretentiousness,
But rather solely out of a wish to maintain the body.

20. Exhortation to Encourage Diligence and Mindfulness

43 (T39)
One should spend the entire day being diligent in his endeavors
And should be so as well in the early and later periods of the night.
One must still maintain mindfulness even in sleeping and dreams,
And must not allow one's life to pass emptily by.

21. On the Four Immeasurable Minds and Cultivating the Dhyāna Absorptions

44 (T40)
Kindness, compassion, sympathetic joy, and right equanimity
Are to be cultivated and are amenable to constant training.
Even though one might not reach the highest level of this practice,
One will nonetheless be able to reborn in the Brahma-world Heaven.²⁸

简体字	正體字
舍杂欲苦寻喜乐 随业当生四地中 大梵光音及遍净 广果天生与彼同	捨雜欲苦尋喜樂 隨業當生四地中 大梵光音及遍淨 廣果天生與彼同
若恒修对治 德胜愍众生 此五行为善 不行为大恶	若恒修對治 德勝愍眾生 此五行為善 不行為大惡
雨盐醎少水 岂若泻江池 纵令微罪业 善大[10]殄应知	雨鹽醎少水 豈若瀉江池 縱令微罪業 善大[10]殄應知
嗔掉举恶作 惛睡欲贪疑 如斯五盖贼 常偷诸善利	嗔掉舉惡作 惛睡欲貪疑 如斯五蓋賊 常偷諸善利
有五最胜法 信勇念定慧 于此应勤习 能招根力顶	有五最勝法 信勇念定慧 於此應勤習 能招根力頂
病苦死爱别 斯皆自业为 未度可勤修 对品[11]亡娇恣	病苦死愛別 斯皆自業為 未度可勤修 對品[11]亡嬌恣

45   (T41)
If, seeking joy and bliss, one renounces the various desires' suffering,
As befits such karma, one may be reborn in any of four stations
Corresponding to the Great Brahma, Light-and-Sound,
Universal Purity, or Extensive Fruition Heavens.²⁹

22. On the Necessity of Cultivating Counteractive Dharmas
46   (T42)
If one constantly cultivates counteractive methods,³⁰
His merit will become supreme and he will feel pity for beings.
These five [countervailing] practices serve as the basis of goodness.
Failing to practice them amounts to the commission of great evil.

23. On the Mitigating Effect of Predominant Goodness
47   (T43)
Sprinkling in a bit of salt to make a little water salty—
How could this be comparable to pouring it into a river or a lake?
Even if one has allowed himself to commit slight karmic offenses,
One should realize they may be mitigated by predominant goodness.

24. On the Destructive Power of the Five Hindrances
48   (T44)
Ill-will, excitedness-and-regretfulness,
Lethargy-and-drowsiness, desire, and doubtfulness—
Insurgent thieves such as these five hindrances
Constantly steal away all benefits of goodness.³¹

25. The Five Root-Faculties, Powers, and Summits
49   (T45)
There are five most superior dharmas:
Faith, vigor, mindfulness, concentration, and wisdom.
One should train diligently in the practice of these.
They are able to beckon forth root-faculties, powers, and summits.

26. Suffering, Its Origin, and Necessity of Right Views to Liberation
A. The Eight Sufferings
50   (T46)
Sufferings of sickness, death, separation from the loved, [and such]—
All of these are creations of one's own karmic deeds.³²
Until one has transcended them, one might well diligently cultivate
Counteractive practices and do away with arrogance and indulgence.

简体字	正體字
若悕天解脱 尔当修正见 设使人行善 邪见招恶果	若悕天解脫 爾當修正見 設使人行善 邪見招惡果
无乐常无我 不净审知人 妄念四倒见 难苦在兹身	無樂常無我 不淨審知人 妄念四倒見 難苦在茲身
说色不是我 我非有于色 色我非更在 知馀四蕴空	說色不是我 我非有於色 色我非更在 知餘四蘊空
不从时节生 非自然本性 非无因自在 [12]从愚业爱生	不從時節生 非自然本性 非無因自在 [12]從愚業愛生
戒禁见身见 及毘织吉蹉 应知三种结 能缚木叉门	戒禁見身見 及毘織吉蹉 應知三種結 能縛木叉門
解脱终依己 不由他伴成 勤修闻戒定 四真谛便生	解脫終依己 不由他伴成 勤修聞戒定 四真諦便生

Chapter 3: *The Yijing Suhṛllekha Translation*

B. The Necessity of Right Views to Liberation

51 (T47)

If you hope to gain the heavens or liberation,
You must then cultivate right views.
Even if one were to influence someone to practice goodness,
Wrong views still result in precipitating wretched karmic effects.

C. The Four Right Views versus the Four Inverted Views

52 (T48)

[By contemplating] absence of bliss, impermanence, absence of self,
And impurity, one analytically cognizes [the nature of] the "person."
Through mentally adopting the four inverted views,
Difficulties and sufferings reside in one's very person.

D. Right and Wrong Views on the Aggregates
1. The Nonexistence of Any "Self" Associated with the Five Aggregates

53 (T49)

It has been declared that form does not constitute a self,
That no self exist as form,
And that it is not true that either form or self abide within the other.[33]
One should realize the other four aggregates are empty [of any self].

2. On the Origins of the Aggregates

54 (T50)

[The aggregates] are not produced by time,
Not produced spontaneously, not produced by their basic nature,
Not produced without a cause, and not created by Īśvara.
They arise as a result of ignorance, karmic action, and craving.[34]

E. Three Fetters Impeding Liberation

55 (T51)

The views implicit in clinging to rules and in conceiving body as self,
And *vicikitsā*, [doubtfulness]—
One should realize these three kinds of fetters
Can tie one up, [preventing entry into] the gate of *mokṣa*, [liberation].

27. The Necessity of Self-Reliance, Learning, Moral Virtue, and Meditation

56 (T52)

Liberation finally depends upon one's own efforts.
It is not realized through association with others.
Diligently cultivate learning, morality, and meditative concentration.
Through which [realization of] the four truths will then develop.

简体字	正體字
增上戒心慧 兹学可常修 百五十馀戒 咸归此三摄	增上戒心慧 茲學可常修 百五十餘戒 咸歸此三攝
于身住身念 兹路善修常 如其亏正念 诸法尽沦亡	於身住身念 茲路善修常 如其虧正念 諸法盡淪亡
寿命多灾厄 如风吹水泡 若得瞬息停 卧起成希有	壽命多災厄 如風吹水泡 若得瞬息停 臥起成希有
卒归灰燥烂 粪秽难久持 观身非实法 灭坏堕分离	卒歸灰燥爛 糞穢難久持 觀身非實法 滅壞墮分離
大地[13]迷卢海 七日出烧燃 况此极微躯 那不成煨烬	大地[13]迷盧海 七日出燒燃 況此極微軀 那不成煨燼
如是无常亦非久 无归无救无家室 生死胜人须厌背 并若芭蕉体无实	如是無常亦非久 無歸無救無家室 生死勝人須厭背 併若芭蕉體無實
海龟投木孔 一会甚难遭 弃畜成人体 恶行果还招	海龜投木孔 一會甚難遭 棄畜成人體 惡行果還招

28. The Three Trainings

57 (T53)

Superior moral virtue, concentration, and wisdom—
These trainings are worthy of constant cultivation.
The more than a hundred and fifty moral precepts
Are all subsumed within these three.³⁵

29. The Station of Mindfulness with Respect to the Body

58 (T54)

Abide in the station of mindfulness with respect to the body.
This is a path worthy of constant skillful cultivation.
If one allows right mindfulness to deteriorate,
All dharmas will be entirely lost.

59 (T55)

One's life is vulnerable to numerous disastrous occurrences.
In this, it is comparable to a water bubble blown by the wind.
When one falls asleep even briefly,
One can only hope that, having lain down, one may yet get up again.

60 (T56)

It will suddenly return to a state of ashes, desiccation, or rot.
This site of feces and filth is difficult to maintain for long.
Contemplate the body as an unreal dharma
Bound for destruction and for disintegration.

61 (T56)

The great earth, Mount Sumeru, and the seas
Will be burned up when the seven suns appear.
How much the more so this extremely fragile body?
How would it not be reduced to cinders?

62 (T58)

Being thus so impermanent, it cannot endure for long.
There is no refuge, no rescue, and no shelter which it might afford.
Whoever would triumph over births and deaths must renounce it.
It is comparable in its insubstantiality to the plantain.³⁶

63 (T59)

Were a sea turtle to poke his head up into a wooden yoke's opening,
That one chance interaction would occur only as an extreme rarity.³⁷
[Equally rare is] casting off animal rebirth to gain the human body.
One may yet return there to encounter the fruits of one's evil actions.

简体字	正體字
金宝[14]盘除粪 斯为是大痴 若生人作罪 全成极惷儿	金寶[14]盤除糞 斯為是大癡 若生人作罪 全成極惷兒
生中依善友 及发于正愿 先身为福业 四大轮全获	生中依善友 及發於正願 先身為福業 四大輪全獲
佛言近善友 全梵行是亲 善士依佛故 众多证圆寂	佛言近善友 全梵行是親 善士依佛故 眾多證圓寂
邪见生鬼畜 泥[15]黎法不闻 边地蔑戾车 生便痴瘂性	邪見生鬼畜 泥[15]黎法不聞 邊地蔑戾車 生便癡瘂性
或生长寿天 除八无暇过 闲暇既已得 尔可务当生	或生長壽天 除八無暇過 閑暇既已得 爾可務當生
爱别老病死 斯等众苦处 智者应生厌 说少过应听	愛別老病死 斯等眾苦處 智者應生厭 說少過應聽
母或改为妇 父乃转成儿 怨家翻作友 迁流无定规	母或改為婦 父乃轉成兒 怨家翻作友 遷流無定規

64 (T60)

To use a tray made of gold and jewels to take out feces
Would be an act of great stupidity.
If, having gained human birth, one were to commit karmic offenses,
He would thereby become the most extreme sort of fool.

30. On the Circumstances Requisite for Cultivating the Path

65 (T61)

With birth into a central land, reliance on the good spiritual friend,[38]
Generation of right vows,
And performance of meritorious karma in one's previous lives,
One has completely acquired all four of the great wheels.[39]

66 (T62)

The Buddha declared of drawing near to the good spiritual friend
And perfecting brahman conduct, one should draw close to these.[40]
Through reliance upon the Buddha, good men
In great numbers have achieved realization of the perfect stillness.[41]

31. Description of the Faults of Cyclic Existence
A. An Introductory General Description of Faults

67 (T63)

One possessed of wrong views is born among the ghosts or animals,
In the hells where he cannot hear the Dharma,
In the hinterlands of the *mleccha*, [the barbarians],
With the facility [for worldly contentiousness], as mute, as deaf,

68 (T64)

Or perhaps he is born in the long-life heavens.[42]
Having set aside these eight unfortunate and faulty circumstances[43]
And having already gained a leisurely situation,
It is fitting that you assume responsibility for your own future births.

69 (T65)

Separation from the loved, ageing, sickness, and death—[44]
This is the abiding place for these and many other sorts of sufferings.
The wise should generate renunciation for it.
You should listen as I describe but a few of its faults:

70 (T66)

[In subsequent births], one's mother may transform into one's wife,
One's father may turn into one's son,
And adversaries may change into friends.
There is no fixed pattern governing the course of transmigrations.

简体字	正體字
一一饮母乳 过于四海水 转受异生身 更饮多于彼	一一飲母乳 過於四海水 轉受異生身 更飲多於彼
过去一一生身骨 展转积若妙高山 地土丸为酸枣核 数己形躯岂尽边	過去一一生身骨 展轉積若妙高山 地土丸為酸棗核 數己形軀豈盡邊
梵主世皆供 业力终沦地 纵绍转轮王 迴身化奴使	梵主世皆供 業力終淪地 縱紹轉輪王 迴身化奴使
三十三天[1]中妓女乐 多时受已堕泥[*]黎 速疾[2]碜毒经诸苦 磨身[3]碎体镇号啼	三十三天[1](中)妓女樂 多時受已墮泥[*]黎 速疾[2]碜毒經諸苦 磨身[3]碎體鎮號啼
妙高岑受乐 地软随其足 转受煻煨苦 行经粪屎狱	妙高岑受樂 地軟隨其足 轉受煻煨苦 行經糞屎獄
欢喜芳园里 天女随游戏 堕落剑林中 截手足耳鼻	歡喜芳園裏 天女隨遊戲 墮落劍林中 截手足耳鼻
或入曼陀妙池[4]浴 天女金花艳彩容 舍身更受泥[*]黎苦 热焰难当灰涧中	或入曼陀妙池[4]浴 天女金花艷彩容 捨身更受泥[*]黎苦 熱焰難當灰澗中

Chapter 3: *The Yijing Suhṛllekha Translation*

71 (T67)
All of the individual instances of drinking one's mothers' milk
Exceed in their volume the four oceans' waters.
Pursuing a common person's destiny, one takes on yet more bodies,
Thus consuming in the future an amount even greater than that.[45]

72 (T68)
The bones from the bodies taken on from each past lifetime,
If piled all together, would rival the height of Mount Sumeru.[46]
Were one to make the entire earth into pellets the size of date pits,
With one for each past body, how could one count them even then?

B. THE IMPERMANENCE AND REVERSIBILITY OF OSTENSIBLY DESIRABLE EXISTENCES

73 (T69)
Having received offerings of everyone as Brahma-World Heaven lord,
When that karma's power ends, one is bound to fall back to earth.
Even if one ascends to the position of a wheel-turning sage king,
Still, on returning, one may be transformed into someone's slave.

74 (T70)
As for the bliss with consorts in the Heaven of the Thirty-three,[47]
After enjoying it for a long time, one may then fall into the hells.
One swiftly meets intense cruelty, enduring all manner of sufferings.
The body is crushed, flesh smashed, one always screams and wails.[48]

75 (T71)
One may experience bliss at the peak of Mount Sumeru.
Where the earth goes soft, cushioning every footstep.
Still, one may turn on back and undergo suffering on burning coals
And then be bound to pass through the hell full of feces.

76 (T72)
One may enjoy delights in the fragrant gardens
Where heavenly maidens follow along in playful rapture.
But then one may fall down into the Sword-Forest Hell
Where one encounters the slicing away of hands, feet, ears, and nose.

77 (T73)
One may enter the marvelous *māndārava* blossom pools to bathe
With heavenly maidens graced by golden flowers and radiant faces.
On leaving that body, one may again endure sufferings in the hells
In fiery blazes hard to confront and in the river of ashes.

简体字	正體字
欲天受法乐 除贪大梵天 更堕阿毘止 薪焰苦恒连	欲天受法樂 除貪大梵天 更墮阿毘止 薪焰苦恒連
或生居日月 身光遍四洲 一朝归黑暗 展手见无由	或生居日月 身光遍四洲 一朝歸黑闇 展手見無由
三种灯明福 死后可持将 独入无边暗 日月不流光	三種燈明福 死後可持將 獨入無邊闇 日月不流光
有命黑绳热 合[5]叫无间下 斯等恒缠苦 烧诸[6]行恶者	有命黑繩熱 合[5]叫無間下 斯等恒纏苦 燒諸[6]行惡者
或若麻床[7][打-丁+此] 或粉如细末 如利[8]斧斫木 犹如锯解割	或若麻床[7][打-丁+此] 或粉如細末 如利[8]斧斫木 猶如鋸解割
猛火恒煎煮 令饮热铜浆 驱令上剑刺 叉身热铁床	猛火恒煎煮 令飲熱銅漿 驅令上劍刺 叉身熱鐵床
或时高举手 铁牙猛狗飡 鹰鸟觜爪利 任彼[9]啅心肝	或時高舉手 鐵牙猛狗飡 鷹鳥觜爪利 任彼[9]啅心肝

78 (T74)
In the desire heavens, one enjoys pleasures consistent with Dharma
And one transcends cravings in the Great Brahma Heaven.
Still, one may plunge down yet again into the Avīci Hells
Where the sufferings of the flames continue on constantly.

79 (T75)
One may be reborn as one who dwells [as a deity] of the sun or moon
Where the body's radiance illuminates throughout four continents.
Still, one is bound one morning to return to that blackness
So intense one has no way to see even his own outstretched hand.

80 (T76)
The lamp light from three types of merit
May be retained and taken along after one's death
As one enters alone the boundless darkness
Wherein the sun and moon do not stream forth their light.[49]

C. The Hells

81 (T77)
The Living Hells, Black-Line Hells, Burning Hells—
The Unification, Screaming, and Non-Intermittent Hells below—
These sorts of constantly engulfing sufferings
Roast all who course in evil deeds.

82 (T78)
They may be crushed on a bed into particles the size of sesame seeds,
Or may be pulverized till they become like finely-ground flour.
Or they may be hacked up just as a sharp axe chops away at logs,
Or else they may be ripped open as if by saws.

83 (T79)
They are subjected to fierce flames which constantly fry and cook,
Are forced to drink molten copper liquid,
Are driven along and forced to fall onto impaling swords,
And have their bodies speared and forced down onto a hot iron bed.

84 (T80)
At times they may raise their hands up high, [pleading],
Only to be set upon by fierce iron-fanged dogs who devour them.
Raptors with sharp beaks and talons [descend upon them]
Forcing them to endure stabbing pecks at the heart and liver.

简体字	正體字

虻蝇及诸虫
其数过千亿
[10]利觜噆身躯
急堕皆飡食

若人具造众罪业
闻苦身[11]自不干堕
如此顽駴金刚性
气尽泥犁遭猛火

时观尽变闻应念
读诵经论常寻鞫
泥犁听响已惊惶
如何遭当斯异熟

于诸乐中谁是最
爱尽无生乐最精
于众苦内谁为极
无间泥犁苦极成

人间一日中
屡刺三百槊
比地狱轻苦
毫分宁相[12]捅

此处受极苦
经百俱胝秋
如其恶未尽
命舍定无由

如是诸恶果
种由身语心
尔勤随力护
轻尘恶勿侵

虻蠅及諸虫
其數過千億
[10]利觜噆身軀
急墮皆飡食

若人具造眾罪業
聞苦身[11]自不干墮
如此頑駴金剛性
氣盡泥犁遭猛火

時觀盡變聞應念
讀誦經論常尋鞫
泥犁聽響已驚惶
如何遭當斯異熟

於諸樂中誰是最
愛盡無生樂最精
於眾苦內誰為極
無間泥犁苦極成

人間一日中
屢刺三百槊
比地獄輕苦
毫分寧相[12]捅

此處受極苦
經百俱胝秋
如其惡未盡
命捨定無由

如是諸惡果
種由身語心
爾勤隨力護
輕塵惡勿侵

85 (T81)
Horseflies and all manner of other insects,
More than a thousand *koṭīs* in number,
With sharp beaks, consume the body.
They all rush to drop on down and proceed to devour it.

86 (T83)
If someone commits in full measure the many sorts of offense karma,
Yet, on hearing of the sufferings, finds no peril therein for himself,
Such a person possesses obdurate stupidity as impenetrable as *vajra*.
When his breath stops, he enters the hells and meets their fierce fires.

87 (T84)
Ever ponder the end's changes. Having learned of them, be mindful.
Study and recite sutras and treatises, always probing their meanings.
Having heard echoes of the hells, struck with terror, one wonders:
"How might one banish or fend off this ripening of karma?"

88 (T85)
Of all the forms of bliss, which is most supreme?
Bliss from ending desire, ensuring its non-arising, is the most refined.
Of all forms of suffering, which is most extreme?
The sufferings of the Non-Intermittent Hells reach the very extreme.

89 (T86)
If every day someone
Were impaled three hundred times with a spear,
That would be but minor suffering compared to that of the hells.
Being but a miniscule fraction of that, one would prefer impalement.

90 (T87)
One may undergo extreme sufferings in these places
Wherein one is bound to pass through a hundred *koṭīs* of years.
So long as one's evil karma had not yet been exhausted,
There would certainly be no way to bring one's life there to an end.

91 (T88)
All such negative fruitions as these
Arise from seeds planted through physical, verbal, and mental acts.
You should diligently guard your actions as best befits your powers.
One must not commit any infractions even as slight as a dust mote.

简体字	正體字
或入傍生趣 杀缚苦恒亲 远离于寂善 更互被艰辛	或入傍生趣 殺縛苦恒親 遠離於寂善 更互被艱辛
或被杀缚苦 求珠尾角皮 锥鞭钩[13]斲顶 踏拍任他骑	或被殺縛苦 求珠尾角皮 錐鞭鉤[13]斲頂 踏拍任他騎
受鬼望不遂 无敌苦常临 饥渴及冷热 困怖苦恒侵	受鬼望不遂 無敵苦常臨 飢渴及冷熱 困怖苦恒侵
口小如针孔 腹大等山丘 饥缠纵己粪 得少定无由	口小如針孔 腹大等山丘 飢纏縱己糞 得少定無由
形如枯杌树 皮方作衣服 炬口夜夜然 飞蛾[14]堕充食	形如枯杌樹 皮方作衣服 炬口夜夜然 飛蛾[14]墮充食
血脓诸不净 福少获无从 更相口排逼 还飡瘿熟痈	血膿諸不淨 福少獲無從 更相口排逼 還飡癭熟癰
月下便招热 日中身遂寒 望菓唯空树 瞻江水剩乾	月下便招熱 日中身遂寒 望菓唯空樹 瞻江水剩乾

D. The Animals

92 (T89)
One may yet enter into the path of animal rebirth
Wherein one personally experiences being bound and slaughtered.
Once one abandons the goodness leading to quiescent cessation,
He is bound to undergo reciprocal infliction of intense bitterness.[50]

93 (T90)
One may be subjected to the sufferings of bondage and slaughter
Arising from quests for pearls, tails, horns, or pelts.
One may be goaded, whipped, hooked, have horns chopped off,
Or may be kicked and smacked as one endures being ridden.

E. The Hungry Ghosts

94 (T91)
When reborn as a ghost, one's hopes are never fulfilled
And one abides in constant proximity to matchless sufferings.
One is subjected to hunger, thirst, cold, and heat
While always being invaded by hardships and terror.

95 (T92)
Their throats are as narrow as the eye of a needle,
Whilst their bellies may even grow as big as a mountain.
Hunger so grips them that, even craving to eat their own excrement,
They definitely have no way to get even a small measure of that.[51]

96 (T93)
In appearance, they resemble a withered tree shorn of branches.
It is their own bare skin which serves for them as clothes.
Their mouths flame like torches which burn night after night,
Drawing flying moths to leap in, supplying them some nourishment.

97 (T94)
Not even blood, pus, or the various sorts of impure substances
Can be obtained by them because their merit is so scant.
They hound after each other with their mouths,
Turning on each other to feast on their ulcerating goiters.

98 (T95)
When exposed to moonlight, they experience feverish heat,
While, when out in the sunshine, they are afflicted with frigid cold.
Though they might hope to eat some fruit, they find only bare trees.
If they look longingly at river waters, all traces of moisture dry up.

简体字	正體字
如是受众苦 经万五千年 长时[15]击身命 良由苦器坚	如是受眾苦 經萬五千年 長時[15](擊)[繫]身命 良由苦器堅
若生饥鬼中 遭斯一味苦 非贤澁者爱 佛说由悭垢	若生飢鬼中 遭斯一味苦 非賢澁者愛 佛說由慳垢
生天虽受乐 福尽苦难思 终归会坠堕 勿乐可应知	生天雖受樂 福盡苦難思 終歸會墜墮 勿樂可應知
厌坐衣沾垢 身光有变衰 [16]液下新流汗 头上故花萎	厭坐衣沾垢 身光有變衰 [16](液)[腋]下新流汗 頭上故花萎
如斯五相现 天众死无疑 地居人若卒 闷乱改常仪	如斯五相現 天眾死無疑 地居人若卒 悶亂改常儀
若从天处堕 众善尽无馀 任落傍生鬼 泥犁[17]随一居	若從天處墮 眾善盡無餘 任落傍生鬼 泥犁[17]隨一居
阿苏罗本性 纵令全觉慧 忿天生苦心 趣遮于见谛	阿蘇羅本性 縱令全覺慧 忿天生苦心 趣遮於見諦

Chapter 3: *The Yijing Suhṛllekha Translation* 149

99 (T96)
They endure manifold sufferings in this manner,
Passing through a period of fifteen thousand years.
That their lives are tied to misery for so very long
Is especially because they are such solid reservoirs of suffering.⁵²

100 (T97)
If one is born among the hungry ghosts,
One encounters this singular flavor of suffering.
It not such as even a worthy ascetic could be fond of.
The Buddha declared it to be caused by the defilement of miserliness.

F. The Gods

101 (T98)
Although one enjoys bliss when born in the heavens,
Once the merit is exhausted, the ensuing suffering is inconceivable.
When the end comes, one plummets back down again.
One may deduce why there is no pleasure to be found in that.

102 (T99)
They become weary of their seats, their clothes become stained,
The luster of their bodies deteriorates,
Their armpits begin to perspire,
And their aging floral chaplets start to wither.⁵³

103 (T100)
When these five signs manifest,
There is no doubt that those among the gods are about to die.
This is just as when earth-bound humans about to die,
Become depressed and scattered and alter their normal deportment.

104 (T101)
If on falling from the abodes of the gods,
All roots of goodness have been entirely exhausted,
One becomes bound to descend into the realms of animals, ghosts,
And hells, abiding then in one after the other.

G. The Asuras

105 (T102)
The basic nature of the *asuras*, [the demigods],
Even when endowed with a full measure of intelligence,
Is to cherish hatred of the gods and generate embittered thoughts.
The effect of this is that it obstructs the ability to perceive the truths.⁵⁴

简体字	正體字
如是漂流生死[18]处 天人畜及阿苏罗 下[19]贱业生众苦器 鬼趣兼投捺落迦	如是漂流生死[18]處 天人畜及阿蘇羅 下[19]賤業生眾苦器 鬼趣兼投捺落迦
纵使烈火燃头上 遍身衣服焰皆通 此苦无暇能除拂 无生住想涅盘中	縱使烈火燃頭上 遍身衣服焰皆通 此苦無暇能除拂 無生住想涅槃中
尔求尸罗及定慧 寂静调柔离垢殃 涅盘无尽无老死 四大日月悉皆亡	爾求尸羅及定慧 寂靜調柔離垢殃 涅槃無盡無老死 四大日月悉皆亡
念择法勇进 定慧喜轻安 此七菩提分 能招妙涅盘	念擇法勇進 定慧喜輕安 此七菩提分 能招妙涅槃
无慧定非有 [20]缺定慧便溺 若其双运者 有海如牛迹	無慧定非有 [20]缺定慧便溺 若其雙運者 有海如牛跡
十四不记法 日亲之所说 于此勿应思 不能令觉灭	十四不記法 日親之所說 於此勿應思 不能令覺滅

H. Summation on Cyclic Existence
106 (T103)
One flows like this through the stations of cyclic births and deaths,
Being born as a god, a human, an animal, or an *asura*, [a demigod].
Base karmic actions are a reservoir producing manifold sufferings.
Those coursing in the path of ghosts are also flung on into the hells.

32. Exhortation to Pursue the Path with Vigor
107 (T104)
It is just as when an intense flame burns [the turban] atop one's head
And threatens to burn all the clothes worn upon one's body.
This suffering is such one brooks no delay in the ability to put it out.
No thought is lost on arising or abiding. It is all focused on nirvāṇa.

33. Encouragement to Cultivate the Three Trainings and Seek Nirvāṇa
108 (T105)
You should seek to practice *śīla* as well as concentration and wisdom.
Develop pliancy through stillness, leaving the disaster of defilements.
Nirvāṇa is endless and free of both ageing and death.
Even the four elements, the sun, and moon all perish there within it.

34. The Seven Limbs of Enlightenment
109 (T106)
Mindfulness, dharmic analysis, vigor,
Meditative concentration, wisdom, joy, and buoyant mental ease—
These seven limbs of bodhi
Are able to bring forth the sublime nirvāṇa.[55]

35. On the Necessity and Decisive Effect of Skill in Meditation and Wisdom
110 (T107)
In the absence of wisdom, meditative absorption is nonexistent.
If meditative absorption is incomplete, wisdom is therefore weak.
In the case of one who implements them both,
The sea of existence becomes like a mere puddle in a bull's hoof print.

36. Avoidance of the Fourteen Indeterminate Dharmas
111 (T108)
The fourteen indeterminate dharmas[56]
Were declared by [the Buddha], the kinsman of the Solar Clan,
To be such as one should not bother to ponder,
For they cannot facilitate either awakening or [nirvāṇa's] cessation.

简体字	正體字
从无知起业 由业复生识 识缘于名色 名色生六处	從無知起業 由業復生識 識緣於名色 名色生六處
六处缘于触 触生缘于受 受既缘于爱 由爱招于取	六處緣於觸 觸生緣於受 受既緣於愛 由愛招於取
取复缘于有 有复缘于生 生缘于老死 忧病求不得	取復緣於有 有復緣於生 生緣於老死 憂病求不得
轮迴大苦蕴 斯应速断除 如其生若灭 众苦[1]珍无馀	輪迴大苦蘊 斯應速斷除 如其生若滅 眾苦[1](珍)[殄]無餘
最胜言教藏 深妙缘起门 如能正见此 便观无上尊	最勝言教藏 深妙緣起門 如能正見此 便觀無上尊
正见命正念 正定语业思 此谓八圣道 为寂可修治	正見命正念 正定語業思 此謂八聖道 為寂可修治
无由集爱起 托身众苦生 除斯证解脱 八圣道宜行	無由集愛起 託身眾苦生 除斯證解脫 八聖道宜行

37. The Twelve-Fold Chain of Causes and Conditions

112 (T109)
It is from ignorance that one generates karmic actions
And from karmic actions that one in turn produces consciousness.
Consciousness is a condition for the production of name-and-form
While it is name-and-form that generates the six sense bases.[57]

113 (T110)
The six sense bases serve as a condition for the production of contact
While it is contact that produces the conditions for feelings.[58]
Feelings having served as a condition for the production of craving,
It is then through craving that one beckons forth grasping.

114 (T111)
Grasping in turn serves as a condition for becoming.
Becoming in turn serves as a condition for birth.
Birth serves as a condition for ageing and death
As well as worry, sickness, and the failure to gain what is sought.

115
As for the great mass of suffering produced by cyclic existence,
This should be swiftly cut off.
If one brings about the cessation of "birth,"
Then the many sorts of suffering are all entirely extinguished.

116 (T112)
Among the treasury of teachings taught by the Supreme One,
This profound and sublime gateway of conditioned arising
Is such that, if one were able to develop correct perception of it,
This would allow one to behold the Unsurpassed Honored One.[59]

38. The Eightfold Path

117 (T113)
Right view and livelihood, right [effort and] mindfulness,
Right meditative discipline, speech, action, and thought—
These are known as the eightfold path of the Āryas.
For the sake of realizing cessation, it is advisable to cultivate them.

39. The Four Truths: Suffering, Accumulation, Cessation, and Path

118 (T114)
The "craving" causing "accumulation" arises baselessly.
It is in dependence on the body that many sorts of "suffering" arise.
It is through "cessation" of this that one realizes liberation.
Hence it is fitting that one practice the Āryas' eightfold "path."[60]

简体字	正體字
即此瑜伽业 四种圣谛因 虽居舍严饰 智遮烦恼津	即此瑜伽業 四種聖諦因 雖居舍嚴飾 智遮煩惱津
不从空处堕 如谷因地造 诸先证法人 皆凡具烦恼	不從空處墮 如穀因地造 諸先證法人 皆凡具煩惱
何假多陈述 除恼略呈言 事由情可伏 圣谈心是源	何假多陳述 除惱略呈言 事由情可伏 聖談心是源
如上所陈法 苾刍难总行 随能修一事 勿令虚夭生	如上所陳法 苾芻難總行 隨能修一事 勿令虛夭生
众善皆随喜 妙行三自修 迴向为成佛 福聚[2]令恒收	眾善皆隨喜 妙行三自修 迴向為成佛 福聚[2]令恒收
后生寿无量 广度于天人 犹如观自在 极难等怨亲	後生壽無量 廣度於天人 猶如觀自在 極難等怨親
生老病死三毒除 佛国托生为世父 寿命时[3]长量叵知 同彼大觉弥陀主	生老病死三毒除 佛國託生為世父 壽命時[3]長量叵知 同彼大覺彌陀主

Chapter 3: *The Yijing Suhṛllekha Translation* 155

III. CONCLUDING EXHORTATORY SECTION

119 (T115)
It is just these very sorts of karmic practices of the yogin
Which serve as the causes for realizing the four truths of the Āryas.[61]
Though one may abide in a household accoutered with adornments,
Wisdom may nonetheless serve to block the stream of afflictions.

120 (T116)
They do not drop down from empty space,
Nor do they grow forth from the earth in the manner of grain.
All who have previously realized the fruits of Dharma
Were formerly common persons replete with afflictions.

121 (T117)
Why tarry in an abundance of explanatory writings?
Dispensing with the toilsome, I submit these summarizing words.
Matters involving individual sentiment are amenable to one's control.
In the discourse of the Āryas, the mind is the source.

122 (T118)
Dharmas such as have been explained above
Would be difficult to comprehensively implement even for a bhikshu.
One may cultivate any given endeavor as befits one's own abilities.
Still, one must not allow one's youth to pass emptily by.

123 (T119)
Accord with and rejoice in all of the many good deeds of others
Pursue the marvelous practice through three types of personal acts.[62]
One should then dedicate these to the realization of buddhahood,
As for the accumulation of merit, see that it is constantly augmented.

124 (T120)
In subsequent lives, one's lifespan may be incalculably long
As one engages extensively in liberating gods and men.
In the manner of Avalokiteśvara,
For those in extreme straits, treat adversaries and friends equally.

125 (T121)
Once free of birth, ageing, sickness, death, and the three poisons,
Manifest birth in your buddhaland to serve the world like a father,
Enjoying an inconceivably long lifespan
Identical to that of the greatly awakened lord, Amitābha.

简体字	正體字
开显尸罗及舍惠 天地虚空名遍彰 大地居人及天众 勿使妖妍女爱伤 烦恼羁缠有情众 绝流生死登正觉 超度世间但有名 由获无生离尘浊	開顯尸羅及捨惠 天地虛空名遍彰 大地居人及天眾 勿使妖妍女愛傷 煩惱羈纏有情眾 絕流生死登正覺 超度世間但有名 由獲無生離塵濁
阿离野那伽曷树那菩提萨埵苏颉里[4]蜜离佉。了	阿離野那伽曷樹那菩提薩埵蘇頡里[4]蜜離佉。了
(阿离野是圣。那伽是龙是象。曷树那义翻为猛。菩提萨埵谓是觉情。苏颉里即是亲密。离佉者书也。先云龙树者讹也)	(阿離野是聖。那伽是龍是象。曷樹那義翻為猛。菩提薩埵謂是覺情。蘇頡里即是親密。離佉者書也。先云龍樹者訛也)
龙树菩萨劝诫王颂	龍樹菩薩勸誡王頌

126　　　　　　　　　　　　　　　　　　　　　　　　　　　　　(T122-3)
Make widely known *śīla*, giving, and wisdom so that throughout
Heavens, earth, and space, their illustriousness is everywhere shown.
Whether among people in the world in celestial congregations,
Do not allow lust for bewitchingly beautiful women to cause harm.
127
The afflictions bind and entwine the multitude of beings.
Cut off the floods of *saṃsāra* and ascend to the right enlightenment.[63]
Step beyond this world consisting of mere designations.
By realizing the unproduced, abandon the turbidity of sense objects.[64]

The End of Ārya Nāgārjuna Bodhisattva's *Suhṛllekha*

An editorial note added to the Chinese text comments on the above line:
"An *ārya* is 'a holy person.' A *nāga* is a 'dragon.' This is an image. The meaning of *arjuna* translates as 'valorous.' A *bodhisattva* is 'an enlightenment being.' As for *suhṛl*, that is 'a close confidante.' As for *lekha*, that means 'letter.' As for earlier statements referring to [the meaning as] 'dragon tree,' those were made in error."

Nāgārjuna Bodhisattva's Verses Exhorting and Admonishing the King

(The end of the Tripiṭaka Master Yijing translation.)

Endnotes to the Yijing Edition

1. As noted in the introduction to this volume, although the king in question here may indeed have been a "friend" of Nāgārjuna in the loose sense of the term, it is Nāgārjuna who adopts in this letter of instruction the role of the "good spiritual friend" (*kalyāṇa-mitra*) or "spiritual guide" and it is for that reason I render the Sanskrit title, *Suhṛllekha*, as "Letter *from* a Friend," and not as "Letter *to* a Friend" (as has been the case with most of the English translations originating with the Tibetan). Indeed, it is Nāgārjuna who is the ārya, not the King. Only an ārya can be relied upon to be one's friend in this and all future lives. The king, "friend" that he might be for the time being, might just as easily change into a deadly enemy with a change of circumstances (say, were he to convert to another religions, for instance) or a change of lifetimes. I suppose it should be noted that there is nothing in the Sanskrit title which defines it as intending either "from" or "to." Restricting it to one interpretation or the other is an artifact of having to produce a rendering into English.
2. It's unclear whether *Chengtu* is an attempted transliteration of "Andhra" or "Guntur" or not a transliteration at all, but rather an attempt at a translation. Guntur District is the 11,000 square kilometer district in which Amaravati is located, the earliest archeological record for it being called "Guntur" being from about 900CE (about 250 years after Yijing's translation). "Andhra" is the much larger Indian state of Andhra Pradesh, known as "Andhra Kingdom" from hundreds of years before Nāgārjuna's lifetime.
3. "Amaravati" is my mildly conjectural Sanskrit reconstruction of the Chinese transliteration characters supplied by the text, this in part based on the sounds those transliteration characters likely had during the Tang Dynasty when Yijing made this translation. Amaravati was the capital of the Sātavāhanas, one of the kings of which is the individual primarily being addressed by Nāgārjuna in this "letter." It seems impossible to know for sure to which of the Sātavāhana kings this work is addressed or if it is the same king addressed by Nāgārjuna's 500-*śloka Ratnāvalī*. Although the Guṇavarman translation of this work addresses its very first verse to "King Satakarni," that is not really so very helpful, this because a number of the Sātavāhana kings bore that name during the course of the five-hundred-year period from about 250BCE to about 250CE.
4. The first half of this verse is legitimately assignable to Nāgārjuna,

based on both Yijing and Guṇavarman. Guṇavarman's translation frames it and translates it as authored by Nāgārjuna:

> Everyone is blanketed and obstructed by ignorance.
> I wish for their sakes to allow benefit to flourish.
>
> (T35.1672.745b16)

5. This second half of the stanza is the "one stanza line," referenced in the Chinese textual note as authored by someone other than Nāgārjuna. It is unclear whether or not the textual note was written by Yijing.
6. N makes it clear elsewhere (In *Mppu*, in his discussion of the recollections) that this refers not just to "giving," but also to the "giving up" or "relinquishing" of the afflictions.
7. This is a standard list known as the "six recollections." The "recollections" vary in the number of components taught. For example, in *Mppu*, N explains that sutra's list of "eight recollections" which, in addition to these six, includes "the breath," and "death." See my translation of *Nāgārjuna on the Eight Recollections*.
8. The ten good karmic deeds involve abstention from: killing, stealing, sexual misconduct (the three of the body), lying, harsh speech, divisive speech, lewd or frivolous speech (the four of the mouth), covetousness, hatefulness, and wrong views (the three of the mind). N elsewhere (in his commentary on the ten bodhisattva grounds) holds forth on the path of the ten good karmic deeds at great length, pointing that they are the basis for the realization of all of the fruits of the Buddhist paths up to and including buddhahood.
9. "Twice-born" refers to members of the Brahmin, Kṣatriya, and Vaiśya castes of Hinduism who have come of age religiously, this through having gone through a ceremony something like Christian "confirmation" or Jewish "bar mitzvah" whereby they then become authorized to learn Sanskrit, study the Vedas, carry out Vedic ceremonies, etc.
10. Although the text might as easily be construed as recommending that the recipients of one's giving will become one's close companions in future lives (which indeed they will, this by virtue of the karmic affinities thus established), the three other editions of the text make it clear that it is the practice of giving itself which alone has the ability to serve as one's true friend in future lives, this because it bestows so many future life benefits. Hence, in translating, I have opted for this equally-defensible but more metaphoric construal of the text's intent.
11. "Sea of existences" refers to all of the stations within the "three realms." "Three realms" is a reference to the desire realm, form realm, and formless realm which in turn contain within them roughly thirty stations of existence ranging from the hells at the bottom of the desire

realm on up through the stations of hungry ghosts, animals, humans, the six desire-realm heavens, sixteen form-realm heavens corresponding to the four dhyānas, and four formless realm heavens corresponding to the formless absorptions of limitless space, limitless consciousness, nothing whatsoever, and the station of neither perception nor non-perception.

12. Obviously, sexual relations within the bounds of marriage is not proscribed for householders. The reference here is to short-term voluntary training for lay people through the skillful means of the eight precepts, usually taken only for single day or, alternately for six set days each month. See the very specific note which follows.

13. These eight precepts constitute the layperson's training regimen in the observance of enhanced moral virtue. They are commonly observed according to three different patterns, this after formally accepting them in a bhikshu-administered ceremony: for one day only, from the first to the fifteenth day of the twelfth lunar month, or, in the more standard form known as the *upavāsa*, on the eighth, fourteenth, fifteenth, twenty-third, twenty-ninth, and thirtieth days of each lunar month. See my translation of *Nāgārjuna on the Perfection of Moral Virtue* for a more extended discussion of all of the specifics involved in the eight-precepts *upavāsa*.

14. Yijing is somewhat inclined to use formal language wherein imperatives are softened when addressing those of high social station. Hence we see the use of "could" instead of the "should" found in other editions.

15. Sundarananda, formerly intractably attached to sensual enjoyments, renounced them after the Buddha showed him the long-term karmic effects, whereupon his cultivation led him to arhatship.

16. Aṅgulimāla was searching for his one-thousandth murder victim when the Buddha brought him to his senses, whereupon he gained arhatship.

17. Kṣemadarśin is another name of Ajātaśatru who is famous for having killed his father to gain the throne. He confessed his crime to the Buddha and developed strong faith in the Dharma.

18. "Non-returner" refers specifically to third-stage arhatship.

19. Although the literal meaning of the Chinese characters (不淨) is in fact "impurity," that is oftentimes a mere "stock" translation adopted by Sino-Buddhism for the Sanskrit *aśubha* which means "unlovely." In the absence of any proof of the actual Sanskrit antecedents here, it doesn't hurt to employ both concepts in the contemplation. Contemplation of the thirty-two (or thirty-six) parts of the body or of the nine stages of a corpse's deterioration makes both ideas abundantly clear.

20. The transliteration used by YJ clearly indicates the *kimpāka* fruit mentioned in Jain and Hindu texts as outwardly attractive and sweet-tasting on the surface, but which nonetheless contains a deadly poisonous interior. The SV edition instead refers by way of analogy to the *bimba* fruit, a common comparison in traditional Sanskrit literature for beautiful ruby-red lips. The GV edition uses neither analogy.

21. It's common to interpret this common Buddhist analogy as pointing to leprosy, but leprosy is not marked by itching as a cardinal symptom. Also, it is caused by bacteria, not by parasitic mites. The Chinese characters used to translate the Sanskrit in all three editions indicate "scabies" which does indeed involve extreme itching created by the boring of the scabies mite and the ensuing allergic reaction.

22. In his *Ratnāvalī* (*Strand of Jewels*), Nāgārjuna makes this idea clearer still:

    0497a17: 如搔癢謂樂不癢最安樂
    0497a18: 如此有欲樂無欲人最樂
    Just as scratching an itch might be thought pleasurable,
    When having no itch is most pleasant of all,
    So too it is with pleasures linked to desire,
    For those free of desire are the happiest of all.
    (寶行王正論 / T25.1656.497a17-8)

23. Nāgārjuna is in no way suggesting that the King should dispense with other recommended practices for accumulating merit and wisdom. He is merely pointing to the superior potency of analytic contemplation in defeating delusions (such as the lust-based attachments just discussed) and in fathoming the ultimate reality of any given phenomenon.

24. Adopting the graphically similar variant found in four other editions (貴 for 責), this because the former is far more likely than the original and also because it accords with the sense of GV, SV, and T. That said, the passage is still interpretable in a somewhat forced manner with the reading offered by *Taisho*, as in: "How would such a person even be worthy of one's reproval?"

25. Emending the text to eliminate the textual corruption which, as it stands, duplicates one of the eight worldly dharmas by including variant Sino-translations of the same dharma (disgrace) while leaving out another (praise).

26. "Muni" is an alternative honorific reference for the Buddha. The relevant meanings in Sanskrit, per the *Monier-Williams Sanskrit-English Dictionary*: "Saint, sage, seer, ascetic, monk, hermit."

    "The seven valuables of the Āryas" (*ārya-dhana*) is a commonly encountered list in both the *Āgamas* and Mahāyāna Sutras.

Chapter 3: *The Yijing Suhṛllekha Translation* 163

27. "Teacher of Gods and Men" (*śāstādeva-manuṣyāṇām*) is another name for the Buddha.
28. These four mind-training states are known as the "four immeasurable minds" (*apramāṇa-citta*) and are also referred to as the "four abodes of Brahmā" (*brahma-vihāra*). For an extensive discussion of this topic and the differences in their cultivation by individual-liberation and universal-liberation practitioners, see my translation of *Nāgārjuna on the Four Immeasurable Minds* under separate cover.
29. This is a reference to cultivation of the four dhyānas. In the first of them, one abandons the suffering of being driven along by the desires characteristic of desire-realm existence and experiences joy and bliss characteristic of that first dhyāna absorption. The particular heavens alluded to in the verse correlate with the form-realm dhyāna heavens.

    Of course rebirth in the heavens is considered to be extremely problematic in Buddhism, this because it only serves to keep one trapped in uncontrolled cyclic births and deaths. Hence it is recommended that one invoke the resolve to follow the path to the Path and instead dedicate all merit to that higher goal which might otherwise conduce to celestial rebirth. This would be equally true of individual-liberation vehicle practitioners and universal-liberation vehicle practitioners.
30. After all is said and done in analyzing this *śloka*, it would seem Yijing's "counteractive methods" and "five [countervailing] practices" are both referring to the five precepts, more or less ignoring the very common "counteractive methods" present in the Guṇavarman edition (impermanence, suffering, emptiness, absence of self, impurity), this because it's not entirely sensible that the failure to incorporate the five most common counteractive modes is somehow necessarily (using the language of Yijing's *śloka*) "tantamount to the commission of great evil." Rather it would simply make consistent hewing to goodness a much more difficult task anchored more on recognition of the sensibility of "the golden rule" and a willingness to follow the moral guidelines inherent in the five precepts than on possession of the wisdom of recognizing the conventional reality of impermanence, suffering, emptiness, absence of self, and impurity as applicable to our most cherished objects of attachment.

    That the five precepts are indeed "counteractive" or "countervailing" practices could go without saying, but, lest that not be so obvious to some, we can easily observe that the rule requiring abstention from killing serves to counteract the hatred implicit in the motivation to kill someone. Where it restrains a person from unnecessarily killing some animal for food, it antidotes a deficiency of compassion. The precept against stealing counteracts inordinate greed. The precept against sexual misconduct antidotes inordinate lust. The precept against lying counteracts the temptation to deceive others simply to achieve some form of self-benefit. The precept against indulgence in intoxicants serves to prevent all of the above, delusion, and much more, this because intoxicants tend to loosen the mind from the moorings of common sense and tend as well to diminish the guiding power of one's inherently-present moral compass.

That said, it still does serve a salutary purpose to review the contents of the Guṇavarman editions interpretation more closely as it really goes more deeply to the basis in wisdom on which the precepts are founded. It recites a list of five "counteractive dharmas" (together with three additional redundancies) which amount to a listing of five very familiar "antidotal" or "counteractive" contemplations recommended in nearly all schools to counter what seem to be the top five deluded imputations:

1) Impermanence (includes GV's redundant "bound to destruction," "non-durability");
2) Suffering (includes GV's redundant "absence of bliss");
3) Emptiness of inherent existence;
4) Absence of self;
5) Impurity (often referenced elsewhere in the Canon as "unloveliness").

The above five "counteractive" methods antidote the following five deluded imputations (in same respective order as above):

1) Permanence;
2) Bliss;
3) Dharmas (i.e. "subjective and objective aspects of existence") as inherently existent;
4) Self (or "soul") as inherently existent;
5) Purity (often referenced elsewhere in the Canon as "loveliness"). This final deluded imputation is obviously the one most associated with sexual desire.

The Guṇavarman edition does not tie the number "five" (or any other number) specifically to these five counteractive dharmas, but instead clearly indicates that the "five" is intended to refer to the five precepts. Interestingly, the Saṅghavarman edition does not seem to have this *śloka* at all for it moves directly from the celestial rebirth *śloka* down to the following *śloka* incorporating the "salt in the Ganges" simile.

The Tibetan edition does not even mention "counteractive" dharmas *or* "precepts" but rather incorporates directly into this *śloka* a list of five factors which, by their relative degree of intensity, either mitigate or intensify any particular karmic act, these relating to: frequency of the act, intensity of inclination in performing the act, degree of ability to prevent the act, presence or absence as objects of the act of those who have assisted one in a positive way (such as one's mother, father, teachers, etc.), presence or absence as objects of the act of those possessed of especially refined virtue (such as the Three Jewels, etc.). None of the three Chinese editions make any mention of this list anywhere in their text. The list articulated in the Tibetan edition is certainly a valid indicator of major factors determinative in the relative "weight" of both karmic virtue and karmic error. It's anybody's guess as to whether it's a commentarial interpolation or instead is actually an accurate reflection of Nāgārjuna's intent somehow not showing up in any of the three rather early Chinese editions.

31. Neither the GV or SV editions make direct mention of the five hindrances, though one might well deduce by inference that they are implicitly indicted as primary topics at issue. GV refers to "five erroneous courses of action" (五邪) and makes a similar analogy, that of "stealing away" one's merit. SV refers to the "thieves operating in the darkness of the five aggregates which "steal away the precious jewels of a person's goodness." The Tibetan *does* refer specifically to the five hindrances.

    The five hindrances contain two dual-component hindrances, "lethargy-and-drowsiness" (*styāna-middha*) and "excitedness-and-regretfulness" (*auddhatya-kaukṛtya*).

    On the question of why "lethargy-and-drowsiness" is a dual-component hindrance, Vasubandhu indicates (in Chapter Five of his *Treatise on the Treasury of Analytic Knowledge*) that it is because both "lethargy" and "drowsiness" are nourished by the same five factors and are productive of the same result of mental languor. Pruden, *Abhidharma-kośa-bhāṣyam* (851-2).

    On the question of why "excitedness-and-regretfulness" is a dual-component hindrance, Vasubandhu indicates that it is because both "excitedness" and "regretfulness" are nourished by the same four factors, are starved by the same single factor (calmness), and are productive of the same result of mental agitation. Pruden, *Abhidharma-kośa-bhāṣyam* (852).

32. My bracketed "and the rest" is intended to indicate that the entire list of the eight sufferings is intended to be inferred. They are: birth, aging, sickness, death, estrangement from the loved, proximity to what is hated, inability to gain what one seeks, the suffering inherent in the five aggregates. The GV edition refers specifically to "the eight sufferings."

33. When this YJ edition says: "it is not the case that either form or self abide one within the other," this just a verse-form condensation of:

"Nor does the self exist within form, nor does form exist within the self." The GV edition is more explicit than the other two Chinese editions in articulating all four of the wrong views on any supposed relationship between the form aggregate and some hypothetical "self":

[The Buddha] has declared that form is not self, self is not form,
There is no form in a self, and there is no self in form—
These four ideas are conceived in relation to the form aggregate.
Any link of a "self" to the other aggregates is in all respects the same.
(T32.1672.746b)

34. The text recites here a short list of wrong views on the origins of the phenomena upon which "self" is imputed, then concludes with the most crucial three of the twelve causal links figuring in the perpetuation of a seeming karmic continuity. YJ translates the name of the Īśvara god into Chinese which, if translated in turn into English, would produce the clumsy and distracting "the god Sovereignly Independent" or some such. Hence I simply reconstruct the Sanskrit. Although "aggregates" are not specified in the text, that they are intended is obvious from the previous śloka. Hence I insert them in brackets.

35. "The more than a hundred and fifty moral precepts" is a somewhat awkward attempt by YJ to refer to the complete monastic precepts for the fully ordained Buddhist monk. (The fully-ordained bhikshu carries just over *two* hundred and fifty precepts in all surviving monastic traditions. This does not include the additional bodhisattva precepts involved in Mahāyāna ordinations.)

36. One may pull away the leaves of a plantain one-by-one, seeking to find its core, only to find that, having done that, nothing remains.

37. This analogy originates with the Buddha. There is but one blind turtle and it rises to the surface of the ocean but once every hundred years. There is only one yoke floating randomly around on the world's oceans. The turtle happens to poke its head up in just the right way that it is as if harnessed in it. This describes the difficulty of regaining human rebirth having once fallen down into the realm of animals.

38. A "central land" is for the most part defined as such by the availability of the Dharma and the "good spiritual friend." The "good spiritual friend" (*kalyāṇa-mitra*) is in most cases an artful term of reference for one's guru or "spiritual guide."

39. From the *Dīrgha-āgama Sutra*: "What are the four dharmas of success? They are what are referred to as "the four wheels." The first

is residence in a central land. The second is proximity to the good spiritual friend. The third is being diligently careful [as regards one's karmic actions]. The fourth is having planted the roots of goodness in previous lives." (T01.0001.53b) "Wheels" here represent an analogy to the wheels of a carriage which allow it to move with speed and grace to its destination.

40. "Brahman conduct" (*brahma-cārya*) refers specifically to strict celibacy.
41. "Perfect stillness" is a Chinese translation of the Sanskrit *nirvāṇa*.
42. Abiding in the long-life heavens involves a complete absence of motivation to cultivate the path of liberation and typically results in a plummeting into the wretched destinies once the celestial lifespan comes to an end, this because one's merit has become completely exhausted. This is comparable to spending all of one's savings at an expensive resort, thus sentencing oneself thereafter to the life of a beggar living in a bad neighborhood.
43. The eight difficulties: birth in the hells; birth among the hungry ghosts, birth among the animals, birth on the continent of Uttarakuru (a blissful place largely free of sufferings, but lacking in Dharma); birth in the long-life heavens (of the form and formless realm); being afflicted with blindness, deafness, or muteness; being possessed of a contentious intelligence which bases itself solely in worldly knowledge (thus making oneself a philistine with respect to spiritual priorities).
44. These four sufferings infer the entire list of eight basic sufferings: birth, ageing, sickness, death, separation from what is loved, proximity to what is detested, not obtaining what is sought, the suffering inherent in the five aggregates.
45. That *yisheng* (異生) translates here the Sanskrit *pṛthag-jana* is corroborated by SV's translation of the same line using the more standard *fanfu* (凡夫).
46. Literally: "Marvelously High Mountain," a common Sino-Buddhist translation of Mount Sumeru.
47. I've emended the text by eliminating the *zhong* (中) from the first line. This accords with four other editions of the text and eliminates the complete oddity of having an eight-character line. This doesn't affect the meaning at all.
48. Lest the implications of this *śloka* be misinterpreted, as I understand it, the purgatorial punishments described here are not necessarily inherently connected to the pleasures enjoyed in the heavens, i.e. they are not somehow a result of "sinning" through enjoyment of celestial pleasures. Indeed, they could only be deemed to be so if they were,

karmically-speaking, "sexual misconduct" (i.e. involving adultery, etc.). Rather, the enjoyments experienced in the heavens are a product of merit created in previous existences, which, when it runs out, allows the underlying karmic forces operative in one's karmic continuum to take over once more. Most of us have a tremendous backlog of bad karma which comes into play when the countervailing force of a temporary high tide of merit recedes. Consequently, previous hell karma is then allowed to come into play, resulting in the purgatorial scenario described here.

49. The three types of merit may be considered from two standpoints:

   1) From the standpoint of their causal bases, namely as produced from giving, from moral virtue, and from patience. (Nāgārjuna identifies these first three perfections as the basis for the generation of the "merit provisions" required for the conquest of enlightenment (*bodhi-saṃbhāra*), noting that the last three perfections (vigor, meditative discipline, and wisdom) constitute the causal bases for the "wisdom provision" required for enlightenment. This analysis is found in Nāgārjuna's *Mahā-prajñā-pāramitā-upadeśa* in the 16-chapter section on the six perfections which I have translated in full under separate cover as *Nāgārjuna on the Six Perfections*.

   2) From the standpoint of the three types of karmic action involved in the production of merit, namely via physical actions, verbal actions, and mental actions.

   The Tibetan commentarial tradition speaks of another interpretation (via giving, moral virtue, and meditation). This would seem to be an inferior analysis, however, this because patience is far more inherently productive of merit than meditation. In fact, meditation may actually be an avenue for destruction of merit, depending on how it is utilized and depending also upon the sorts of meditation states toward which one gravitates.

50. "Reciprocal infliction of intense bitterness" refers to killing and eating each other.

51. Hungry ghosts feed on all manner of impure substances such as excrement, snot, spittle, pus, and so forth.

52. Adopting the graphically similar variant found in four other editions (繫 in place of 擊), this because the replacement character is far more likely to represent the original reading. That said, the passage is still interpretable with the reading offered by *Taisho*, as in: "That their lives are for so long stricken by them...."

   Lest the meaning here seem obscure, the metaphor "because they are such solid reservoirs of suffering..." refers to the retribution-

Chapter 3: *The Yijing Suhṛllekha Translation*

related circumstance set up for the hungry ghost by their own past-life miserliness. The result: An unbreakably solid outcome in the present necessarily involving long-term privation and suffering.

53. Adopting the graphically similar variant found in four other editions (腋 for 液), this to correct an obvious scribal error.

54. "Truths" here is a reference to the four truths (suffering, its origination, its cessation, the path to its cessation), the direct perception of which is key to realization of the fruits of all Buddhist Paths.

55. Perhaps one should be aware that the seven limbs of bodhi vary somewhat from text to text in the way they are listed. Basically, they are: dharmic analysis, vigor, joy, buoyant mental ease (*praśrabdhi*), mindfulness, concentration, and, depending on the scripture, either "wisdom," or the "equanimity" associated with the formative-factor aggregate (as opposed to the equanimity with regard to the "feelings" aggregate which is so important in the acquisition of the dhyānas). The role of formative-factor equanimity in wisdom should be fairly obvious, however. Hence the difference between the two lists is relatively insignificant.

56. The fourteen are: Are the World and the self eternal, non-eternal, both, or neither?; Do the World and the self come to an end, or not, or both, or neither?; Does the Buddha continue to exist after his nirvāṇa, or not, or both, or neither?; Are the body and the soul identical or different? The Buddha deemed that answering these questions would serve no purpose, not least because they were like asking, "How much milk can one obtain from tugging on a bull's horn?" and hence would not conduce toward awakening.

57. "Name-and-form" is a term referencing the mental ("name") and physical ("form") aggregates upon which personhood is typically imputed.

58. "Feeling" is of six types corresponding to the six sense faculties. It is often misconstrued as referencing just physical sensation or just emotional "feelings." In fact it refers to both. Vasubandhu makes this quite clear in his *Abhidharma-kośa-bāṣyam*.

59. Lest it not be obvious, "Supreme One" and "Unsurpassed Honored One" are both direct references to the Buddha.

60. One will notice that the simple logic behind the four truths is described in this *śloka*, wherein the "craving" link in the twelve-fold causal chain is indicated as at the same time key to the generation of suffering and also key to its cessation.

61. "Karmic practices of the yogin" refers specifically to the above-discussed cultivation of the seven limbs of bodhi, practice of both wisdom and meditation, non-involvement with the fourteen indeterminate

theorizations, contemplation of the twelve-fold causal chain, practice of the eightfold path, and so forth.
62. "Three types of personal acts" refers to one's own actions of body, mouth, and mind.
63. The SV translation specifies "the four floods" (*catur-ogha*). These are: views (*dṛṣṭi-ogha*), desire (*kāma-ogha*), "becoming / existence" (*bhava-ogha*), and ignorance (*avidyā-ogha*).
64. "Unproduced" is a reference to the "unproduced dharmas patience" (*anutpattika-dharma-kṣānti*).

Source Text Variant Readings

Guṇavarman Translation:

[0745001] 罽賓三藏＝三藏法師【宋】【元】【明】【宮】
[0745002] 垂＝乘【宮】
[0745003] 殖＝植【宋】【元】【明】【宮】下同
[0745004] 間＝聞【宋】【宮】
[0745005] 瞋＝憍【宋】【元】【明】【宮】
[0745006] 妄＝忘【明】，＝空【宮】
[0746001] 士＝上【宮】
[0746002] 證＝登【宮】
[0746003] 二＝三【明】
[0746004] 盛＝益【明】
[0746005] 當＝常【宋】【元】【明】【宮】
[0746006] 能＝解【宋】【元】【明】【宮】
[0746007] 有＝得【宋】【元】【明】【宮】

正體字

Guṇavarman Translation

[0745001] 罽宾三藏＝三藏法师【宋】【元】【明】【宫】
[0745002] 垂＝乘【宫】
[0745003] 殖＝植【宋】【元】【明】【宫】下同
[0745004] 间＝闻【宋】【宫】
[0745005] 瞋＝憍【宋】【元】【明】【宫】
[0745006] 妄＝忘【明】，＝空【宫】
[0746001] 士＝上【宫】
[0746002] 证＝登【宫】
[0746003] 二＝三【明】
[0746004] 盛＝益【明】
[0746005] 当＝常【宋】【元】【明】【宫】
[0746006] 能＝解【宋】【元】【明】【宫】
[0746007] 有＝得【宋】【元】【明】【宫】

简体字

<table>
<tr><td rowspan="18">正體字</td><td>[0746008] 精＝勤【宮】</td></tr>
<tr><td>[0746009] 法＝處【宋】【元】【明】</td></tr>
<tr><td>[0746010] 滅＝減【宋】【元】【明】</td></tr>
<tr><td>[0746011] 乾＝就【宮】</td></tr>
<tr><td>[0746012] 常＝當【宋】【元】【明】【宮】</td></tr>
<tr><td>[0746013] 見知＝知見【宋】【元】【明】【宮】</td></tr>
<tr><td>[0746014] 憎＝增【明】</td></tr>
<tr><td>[0747001] 生＝坐【宋】【元】【明】【宮】</td></tr>
<tr><td>[0747002] 使＝役【宋】【元】【明】【宮】</td></tr>
<tr><td>[0747003] 地＝池【明】</td></tr>
<tr><td>[0747004] 或＝如【明】</td></tr>
<tr><td>[0747005] 押＝壓【宋】【元】【明】【宮】＊［＊1］</td></tr>
<tr><td>[0747006] 支＝肢【宋】【元】【明】【宮】</td></tr>
<tr><td>[0747007] 今＝令【宋】【元】【明】【宮】</td></tr>
<tr><td>[0747008] 鳥＝烏【宮】</td></tr>
</table>

<table>
<tr><td rowspan="15">简体字</td><td>[0746008] 精＝勤【宫】</td></tr>
<tr><td>[0746009] 法＝处【宋】【元】【明】</td></tr>
<tr><td>[0746010] 灭＝减【宋】【元】【明】</td></tr>
<tr><td>[0746011] 乾＝就【宫】</td></tr>
<tr><td>[0746012] 常＝当【宋】【元】【明】【宫】</td></tr>
<tr><td>[0746013] 见知＝知见【宋】【元】【明】【宫】</td></tr>
<tr><td>[0746014] 憎＝增【明】</td></tr>
<tr><td>[0747001] 生＝坐【宋】【元】【明】【宫】</td></tr>
<tr><td>[0747002] 使＝役【宋】【元】【明】【宫】</td></tr>
<tr><td>[0747003] 地＝池【明】</td></tr>
<tr><td>[0747004] 或＝如【明】</td></tr>
<tr><td>[0747005] 押＝压【宋】【元】【明】【宫】＊［＊1］</td></tr>
<tr><td>[0747006] 支＝肢【宋】【元】【明】【宫】</td></tr>
<tr><td>[0747007] 今＝令【宋】【元】【明】【宫】</td></tr>
<tr><td>[0747008] 鸟＝乌【宫】</td></tr>
</table>

Source Text Variant Readings

正體字

[0747009] 齟＝[齒*盧]【宋】【元】【宮】，＝攄【明】
[0747010] 已＝以【宋】【元】【明】【宮】
[0747011] 鉾[打-丁+(臾-火+焱)]＝矛[矛*(替-曰+貝)]【宋】【元】【明】【宮】
[0747012] 毘＝鼻【宋】【元】【明】【宮】
[0747013] 緣＝終【宋】【元】【明】
[0747014] 墜＝墮【明】
[0747015] 困＝因【宋】【元】【明】【宮】
[0747016] 屎尿＝尿屎【宋】【元】【明】【宮】
[0747017] 涼＝淨【宮】
[0747018] 竭＝渴【宋】【元】
[0747019] 深＝染【宋】【元】【明】【宮】
[0747020] 具＝真【宮】
[0747021] 患＝惡【宋】【元】【明】【宮】
[0747022] [漂*寸]＝漂【宮】

简体字

[0747009] 龃＝[齿*卢]【宋】【元】【宮】，＝攄【明】
[0747010] 已＝以【宋】【元】【明】【宮】
[0747011] 鉾[打-丁+(臾-火+焱)]＝矛[矛*(替-曰+贝)]【宋】【元】【明】【宮】
[0747012] 毘＝鼻【宋】【元】【明】【宮】
[0747013] 缘＝终【宋】【元】【明】
[0747014] 坠＝堕【明】
[0747015] 困＝因【宋】【元】【明】【宮】
[0747016] 屎尿＝尿屎【宋】【元】【明】【宮】
[0747017] 凉＝净【宮】
[0747018] 竭＝渴【宋】【元】
[0747019] 深＝染【宋】【元】【明】【宮】
[0747020] 具＝真【宮】
[0747021] 患＝恶【宋】【元】【明】【宮】
[0747022] [漂*寸]＝漂【宮】

	Saṅghavarman Translation
正體字	[0748001] 僧伽＝求那【宋】【元】【明】
	[0748002] 尊視＝存木【宋】【元】【明】，＝存示【宮】
	[0748003] 光＝宣【宮】
	[0748004] 實＝寶【元】【明】
	[0748005] 邪修＝修邪【宋】【元】【明】【宮】
	[0748006] 田＝由【宋】【元】【宮】
	[0748007] 超＝起【宋】【元】【明】【宮】
	[0748008] 刀＝熾【宮】
	[0748009] 士＝者【宋】【元】【明】
	[0748010] 纓絡＝瓔珞【宮】
	[0749001] 賤＝則【宋】【元】【明】
	[0749002] 夫＝天【宋】【元】【明】
	[0749003] 勤＝覲【宮】
	[0749004] 旋＝迴【宋】【元】【明】【宮】
	Saṅghavarman Translation
简体字	[0748001] 僧伽＝求那【宋】【元】【明】
	[0748002] 尊视＝存木【宋】【元】【明】，＝存示【宫】
	[0748003] 光＝宣【宫】
	[0748004] 实＝宝【元】【明】
	[0748005] 邪修＝修邪【宋】【元】【明】【宫】
	[0748006] 田＝由【宋】【元】【宫】
	[0748007] 超＝起【宋】【元】【明】【宫】
	[0748008] 刀＝炽【宫】
	[0748009] 士＝者【宋】【元】【明】
	[0748010] 缨络＝璎珞【宫】
	[0749001] 贱＝则【宋】【元】【明】
	[0749002] 夫＝天【宋】【元】【明】
	[0749003] 勤＝觐【宫】
	[0749004] 旋＝迴【宋】【元】【明】【宫】

Source Text Variant Readings

[0749005]	怙＝護【宮】
[0749006]	數＝量【宋】【元】【明】【宮】
[0750001]	天＝入【宮】
[0750002]	歡＝歎【宮】
[0750003]	死＝亦【宋】【元】【明】【宮】
[0750004]	八＝入【明】
[0750005]	像＝蒙【宮】
[0750006]	採＝采【宋】【元】【明】【宮】
[0750007]	宜＝其【宋】【元】【明】【宮】
[0750008]	頸＝雄【宮】
[0750009]	調＝訓【宮】
[0750010]	迫＝逼【宋】【元】【明】【宮】
[0750011]	大＝太【宋】【元】【明】【宮】
[0750012]	內＝肉【宋】【元】【宮】
[0750013]	齚＝齝【元】【明】

正體字

[0749005]	怙＝护【宫】
[0749006]	数＝量【宋】【元】【明】【宫】
[0750001]	天＝入【宫】
[0750002]	欢＝叹【宫】
[0750003]	死＝亦【宋】【元】【明】【宫】
[0750004]	八＝入【明】
[0750005]	像＝蒙【宫】
[0750006]	采＝采【宋】【元】【明】【宫】
[0750007]	宜＝其【宋】【元】【明】【宫】
[0750008]	颈＝雄【宫】
[0750009]	调＝训【宫】
[0750010]	迫＝逼【宋】【元】【明】【宫】
[0750011]	大＝太【宋】【元】【明】【宫】
[0750012]	内＝肉【宋】【元】【宫】
[0750013]	齚＝齝【元】【明】

简体字

正體字	[0750014] 瘡＝瘦【宮】 [0750015] 熾＝鐵【明】 [0750016] 逾＝愈【宋】【元】【明】【宮】 [0750017] 復＝墜【宮】 [0750018] 勤＝對【宮】 [0750019] 當＝常【宋】【元】【明】【宮】 [0750020] 則＝即【宋】【元】【明】【宮】 [0750021] 都＝苦【明】【宮】 [0750022] 實＝最【宮】 [0750023] 常＝當【宋】【元】【明】 **Yijing Translation** [0751001] 〔大〕－【明】 [0751002] 土＝士【宋】 [0751003] 愛＝慶【明】 [0751004] 悕＝怖【宋】【元】【明】【宮】
简体字	[0750014] 疮＝瘦【宫】 [0750015] 炽＝铁【明】 [0750016] 逾＝愈【宋】【元】【明】【宫】 [0750017] 复＝坠【宫】 [0750018] 勤＝对【宫】 [0750019] 当＝常【宋】【元】【明】【宫】 [0750020] 则＝即【宋】【元】【明】【宫】 [0750021] 都＝苦【明】【宫】 [0750022] 实＝最【宫】 [0750023] 常＝当【宋】【元】【明】 **Yijing Translation** [0751001] 〔大〕－【明】 [0751002] 土＝士【宋】 [0751003] 爱＝庆【明】 [0751004] 悕＝怖【宋】【元】【明】【宫】

Source Text Variant Readings

[0751005] 說＝語【元】【明】	
[0751006] 宵＝霄【明】	
[0751007] 央＝史【宋】【宮】	
[0751008] 舍＝含【明】	
[0751009] 如＝知【宋】【元】【明】【宮】	
[0751010] 刀＝力【宋】【元】【明】【宮】	
[0752001] 降＝除【宋】【元】【明】【宮】	正體字
[0752002] 仗＝伏【宋】【宮】	
[0752003] 止＝正【宮】	
[0752004] 免＝逸【宋】【元】【明】【宮】	
[0752005] 責＝貴【宋】【元】【明】【宮】	
[0752006] 若＝名【宋】【宮】	
[0752007] 男偶＝勇愚【宋】【明】【宮】	
[0752008] 住＝任【宋】【元】【明】【宮】	
[0752009] 修習＝習修【明】	
[0751005] 说＝语【元】【明】	
[0751006] 宵＝霄【明】	
[0751007] 央＝史【宋】【宮】	
[0751008] 舍＝含【明】	
[0751009] 如＝知【宋】【元】【明】【宮】	
[0751010] 刀＝力【宋】【元】【明】【宮】	
[0752001] 降＝除【宋】【元】【明】【宮】	简体字
[0752002] 仗＝伏【宋】【宮】	
[0752003] 止＝正【宮】	
[0752004] 免＝逸【宋】【元】【明】【宮】	
[0752005] 责＝贵【宋】【元】【明】【宮】	
[0752006] 若＝名【宋】【宮】	
[0752007] 男偶＝勇愚【宋】【明】【宮】	
[0752008] 住＝任【宋】【元】【明】【宮】	
[0752009] 修习＝习修【明】	

正體字	[0752010] 殄＝彌【宋】【宮】 [0752011] 亡嬌＝忘憍【明】 [0752012] 從＝提【明】 [0752013] 迷＝彌【宋】【元】【明】【宮】 [0752014] 盤＝槃【宋】【元】【明】【宮】 [0752015] 黎＝犁【宋】【元】【明】【宮】＊［＊１２］ [0753001] 〔中〕－【宋】【元】【明】【宮】 [0753002] 磣＝躁【宋】【宮】，＝慘【元】【明】 [0753003] 碎＝拭【宋】【元】【明】【宮】 [0753004] 浴＝沼【宋】【宮】 [0753005] 叫＝吽【明】 [0753006] 行惡＝惡行【宋】【元】【明】【宮】 [0753007] ［打-丁+此］＝批【明】 [0753008] 斧斫＝斫斧【宋】【元】【明】【宮】 [0753009] 啅＝啄【宋】【元】【明】【宮】
简体字	[0752010] 殄＝弥【宋】【宫】 [0752011] 亡娇＝忘憍【明】 [0752012] 从＝提【明】 [0752013] 迷＝弥【宋】【元】【明】【宫】 [0752014] 盘＝盘【宋】【元】【明】【宫】 [0752015] 黎＝犁【宋】【元】【明】【宫】＊［＊１２］ [0753001] 〔中〕－【宋】【元】【明】【宫】 [0753002] 碜＝躁【宋】【宫】，＝惨【元】【明】 [0753003] 碎＝拭【宋】【元】【明】【宫】 [0753004] 浴＝沼【宋】【宫】 [0753005] 叫＝吽【明】 [0753006] 行恶＝恶行【宋】【元】【明】【宫】 [0753007] ［打-丁+此］＝批【明】 [0753008] 斧斫＝斫斧【宋】【元】【明】【宫】 [0753009] 啅＝啄【宋】【元】【明】【宫】

Source Text Variant Readings

[0753010]	利＝此【宋】【宮】	
[0753011]	自不干＝肉不千【宋】【宮】，＝肉百千【元】【明】	
[0753012]	捅＝掐【宋】【元】【明】【宮】	
[0753013]	蹔＝蹔【宋】【元】【明】【宮】	
[0753014]	墮＝隨【宋】【元】【明】【宮】	
[0753015]	擊＝繫【宋】【元】【明】【宮】	
[0753016]	液＝腋【宋】【元】【明】【宮】	正體字
[0753017]	隨＝墮【宋】【元】【明】【宮】	
[0753018]	處＝趣【明】	
[0753019]	賤＝殘【宮】	
[0753020]	缺＝決【宋】【元】【明】【宮】	
[0754001]	珍＝殄【宋】【元】【明】【宮】	
[0754002]	令＝爾【宋】【元】【宮】，＝而【明】	
[0754003]	長＝量【宮】	
[0754004]	〔蜜〕－【宋】【元】【明】【宮】	
[0753010]	利＝此【宋】【宮】	
[0753011]	自不干＝肉不千【宋】【宮】，＝肉百千【元】【明】	
[0753012]	捅＝掐【宋】【元】【明】【宮】	
[0753013]	蹔＝蹔【宋】【元】【明】【宮】	
[0753014]	堕＝随【宋】【元】【明】【宮】	
[0753015]	击＝系【宋】【元】【明】【宮】	
[0753016]	液＝腋【宋】【元】【明】【宮】	简体字
[0753017]	随＝堕【宋】【元】【明】【宮】	
[0753018]	处＝趣【明】	
[0753019]	贱＝残【宮】	
[0753020]	缺＝决【宋】【元】【明】【宮】	
[0754001]	珍＝殄【宋】【元】【明】【宮】	
[0754002]	令＝尔【宋】【元】【宮】，＝而【明】	
[0754003]	长＝量【宮】	
[0754004]	〔蜜〕－【宋】【元】【明】【宮】	

About the Translator

Bhikshu Dharmamitra (ordination name "Heng Shou" – 釋恆授) is a Chinese-tradition translator-monk and one of the early American disciples (since 1968) of the late Weiyang Ch'an patriarch, Dharma teacher, and exegete, the Venerable Master Hsuan Hua (宣化上人). He has a total of 23 years in robes during two periods as a monastic (1969–1975; 1991 to present).

Dharmamitra's principal educational foundations as a translator lie in four years of intensive monastic training and Chinese-language study of classic Mahāyāna texts in a small-group setting under Master Hua from 1968–1972, undergraduate Chinese language study at Portland State University, a year of intensive one-on-one Classical Chinese study at the Fu Jen University Language Center near Taipei, and two years at the University of Washington's School of Asian Languages and Literature (1988–90).

Since taking robes again under Master Hua in 1991, Dharmamitra has devoted his energies primarily to study and translation of classic Mahāyāna texts with a special interest in works by Ārya Nāgārjuna and related authors. To date, he has translated a dozen important texts, most of which are slated for publication by Kalavinka Press.

Kalavinka Buddhist Classics Title List

Meditation Instruction Texts

The Essentials of Buddhist Meditation
A marvelously complete classic *śamathā-vipaśyanā* (calming-and-insight) meditation manual. By Tiantai Śramaṇa Zhiyi (538–597 CE).

The Six Gates to the Sublime
The earliest Indian Buddhist meditation method explaining the essentials of breath and calming-and-insight meditation. By Śramaṇa Zhiyi.

Bodhisattva Path Texts

Nāgārjuna on the Six Perfections
Chapters 17–30 of Ārya Nāgārjuna's *Mahāprājñāpāramitā Upadeśa*.

Marvelous Stories from the Perfection of Wisdom
130 stories from Ārya Nāgārjuna's *Mahāprājñāpāramitā Upadeśa*.

A Strand of Dharma Jewels (Ārya Nāgārjuna's *Ratnāvalī*)
The earliest extant edition, translated by Paramārtha: *ca* 550 CE

Nāgārjuna's Guide to the Bodhisattva Path
The *Bodhisaṃbhāra Treatise* with abridged Vaśitva commentary.

The Bodhisaṃbhāra Treatise Commentary
The complete exegesis by the Indian Bhikshu Vaśitva (*ca* 300–500 CE).

Letter from a Friend - The Three Earliest Editions
The earliest extant editions of Ārya Nāgārjuna's *Suhṛlekkha*:
Translated by Tripiṭaka Master Guṇavarman	(*ca* 425 CE)
Translated by Tripiṭaka Master Saṅghavarman	(*ca* 450 CE)
Translated by Tripiṭaka Master Yijing	(*ca* 675 CE)

Resolve-for-Enlightenment Texts

On Generating the Resolve to Become a Buddha
On the Resolve to Become a Buddha by Ārya Nāgārjuna
Exhortation to Resolve on Buddhahood by Patriarch Sheng'an Shixian
Exhortation to Resolve on Buddhahood by the Tang Literatus, Peixiu

Vasubandhu's Treatise on the Bodhisattva Vow
By Vasubandhu Bodhisattva (*ca* 300 CE)

*All Kalavinka Press translations include facing-page source text.

www.ingramcontent.com/pod-product-compliance
Lightning Source LLC
LaVergne TN
LVHW011419080426
835512LV00005B/152